# THE
# COURAGE
# TO BE
# ORDINARY

Also by Ichiro Kishimi:

*The Courage to be Disliked*
*The Courage to be Happy*
*The Courage to Love*
*The Courage to Let Go*
*The Courage to Grow Old*

# THE COURAGE TO BE ORDINARY

**ICHIRO KISHIMI**

Translated by Haydn Trowell

Vermilion

VERMILION

UK | USA | Canada | Ireland | Australia
India | New Zealand | South Africa

Vermilion is part of the Penguin Random House group of companies
whose addresses can be found at global.penguinrandomhouse.com

Penguin Random House UK
One Embassy Gardens, 8 Viaduct Gardens, London SW11 7BW

penguin.co.uk

Original Japanese edition first published in Japan as "FUTSU" NI TSUKERU
KUSURI by Sunmark Publishing in 2025
English edition first published in the UK by Vermilion in 2026

English translation rights arranged with Sunmark Publishing, Inc. through
Japan UNI Agency, Inc., Tokyo and Vicki Satlow of The Agency srl, Milano

2



Typeset in 10.75/16pt Bembo Infant MT Std by
Six Red Marbles UK, Thetford, Norfolk

Printed and bound in Great Britain by Clays Ltd, Elcograf S.p.A.

The authorised representative in the EEA is Penguin Random House Ireland,
Morrison Chambers, 32 Nassau Street, Dublin D02 YH68

A CIP catalogue record for this book is available from the British Library

Hardback ISBN 9781785047046
Trade Paperback ISBN 9781785046773

# CONTENTS


Foreword: The Courage to Be Ordinary     1

Introduction: Letting Go of the Need to Be Special     3

**Chapter 1: Why Do I Believe I Have to Be Special?**     7

Why Comparisons Are a Trap     9

The Day I Stopped Trying to be Special     13

How Birth Order Shapes Our Lifestyle Choices     16

How Parental Approval Feeds the Desire to Be Special     22

The Influence of Parental Values     25

How the 'Special' Mindset Becomes Fixed     27

**Chapter 2: The Fragile Superiority of Those Who Need to Be Special**     29

People Who Are Habitually Tense     31

People Who Feel Crushed by Others' Expectations     33

The Inferiority Behind the Need to Be Special     37

Special People Who Eventually Stumble     39

People Who Want to Be Seen as Special Yet Do Nothing     41

**Chapter 3: What It Means to Be Ordinary**     43

Why You Don't Need to Be Special     45

Ordinary Doesn't Mean Boring     47

When It's Tempting to Follow the Crowd     49

Society Needs People Who Speak Up     52

You Don't Need to Stand Out to Be Different 55

Choose a Life That's Truly Your Own 57

**Chapter 4: Overcoming Feelings of Inferiority** 59

The Illusion of Cause and Effect 61

There Is No Causal Relationship Between
    Education and Ability 62

Academic Background Is Just an Attribute 64

'Anyone Can Accomplish Anything' 66

Inferiority Feelings Stand in the Way of Action 69

Self-manufactured Anxiety Boxes You In 72

Comparing Yourself Now to Your Past Self Stalls Growth 74

You Simply Don't Need Inferiority Feelings 76

You Can Make a Healthy Effort Without
    Feeling Inferior First 79

Why We Always End Up Thinking in Terms of
    Superior and Inferior 82

You Can Change the Way You Think 84

**Chapter 5: Approaching Your Life with Confidence** 87

The Weight Holding You Down Is Self-made 89

Competition Isn't a Given 90

Don't Compare Yourself to Others 92

There's No Need to Compete 95

Losing a Competition Doesn't Erase Your Value 98

Instead of Fearing Failure, Learn How to Handle It 100

Don't Be Afraid of Producing Results 103

Confidence Has Nothing to Do with Competition 105

Don't Say But 107

Don't Live in Possibility                                    108

Focus Only on the Task at Hand                              110

You Don't Need Other People's Approval                      113

The Crushing Weight of Trying to Be Special                 115

Evaluation Doesn't Determine Value                          117

When You *Should* Care About How Others See You             119

Free Yourself from Other People's Expectations              121

Asking for Other People's Cooperation                       124

Doing *Good* Work                                           127

Doing Work That Only You Can Do                             129

Listening to Your Vocation                                  133

## Chapter 6: Starting from Who You Are                      137

Accepting the Real You                                      139

Knowing That You Don't Know                                 142

You Can Only Start from What You Can Do                     144

Moving Beyond Fear Towards Growth                           146

Have the Courage to Accept That You Can
    Always Know More                                        148

Stop Trying to Make Yourself Look Better
    Than You Are                                            150

Stop Being Preoccupied with Yourself                        153

Don't Let Anyone Else Decide What You Can
    and Can't Do                                            155

Enjoy the Process of Learning                               157

Learn Slowly                                                159

Start Something New                                         162

Value the Process, Not Just the Outcome                     165

**Chapter 7: Living Your Own Life**     **169**

Being Ordinary in Relationships     171

Stumbling in Relationships     172

Self-worth Is the Doorway to Every Relationship     174

Making Use of Who You Already Are     177

The Importance of Making Your Own Choices     180

Don't Try to Become Special Just to Be Accepted     183

Don't Be Afraid to Be Different from Everyone Else     185

Have Confidence in Being Yourself     188

Embrace Individuality     191

An Irreplaceable Individuality     193

Stop Thinking Only of Yourself     195

Taking an Interest in Others and Working Together     198

Winning Alone Is Meaningless     201

Gaining a Sense of Belonging     203

It Isn't Give and Take     205

Use Your Talents to Contribute to Others     208

You Contribute Simply by Existing     211

The Important Things in Life     214

Living Happily     217

**Conclusion: Finding the Courage to Be Ordinary**     **219**

People with Real Confidence Don't Rush     221

Being an Ordinary Person     223

Works Cited     225

# FOREWORD

## The Courage to Be Ordinary

You may have heard the saying 'There's no cure for stupidity.' But is there a cure for being ordinary?

This book grew out of a conversation I had with a young man not too long ago. 'I'm starting to think I'm more ordinary than I believed,' he told me. 'I don't know if I can come to terms with not being special.' The restless unease behind his words was the same anxiety that quietly gnaws at so many of us.

You thought you were one of the capable ones in school or at work, and then suddenly, you're not so sure.

Maybe you'll never be number one. Maybe you won't even be another person's one and only.

This book, *The Courage to Be Ordinary*, is written for anyone who has ever felt that fear.

What I want to show you here is how to live happily without having to compete with anyone.

At the root of the fear of not being special lies endless comparison. For so many of us, life turns into constant competition, where we can't truly relax unless we feel undefeated. But chasing victory like this – the pursuit of the elusive feeling of being special – keeps us living with our shoulders permanently tensed.

How do we free ourselves from comparison? How do we reclaim our confidence and start living a genuinely happy life?

In these pages, we'll explore a way of living best summed up as *not trying to be special, yet not becoming a copy of everyone else.*

Let's begin the journey of letting go of tension, of comparison and of fear.

# INTRODUCTION
## Letting Go of the Need to Be Special

Maybe you were the kid with top grades, or the young professional who always produced results and earned the respect of everyone around you. Yet even you might suddenly wonder, 'Can I really keep performing like this for the rest of my career?'

Perhaps you already know the sting of losing confidence – the realisation that you might not be as exceptional as you once believed. Maybe you still think of yourself as talented, but worry that one day a more capable rival will appear and shake your throne.

If you've spent your life believing you're special, then the idea of being ordinary can feel unbearable. But *why* do we feel like we have to be special? Why isn't it okay just to be ordinary? This book is for those who feel they must constantly be exceptional.

By the time you finish reading, I hope you'll no longer feel the need to think, *I have to be special*, or *I refuse to be ordinary*, and that you'll start to release the pent-up strain that's been running your life.

I should tell you, though, that there's no quick fix. It takes courage to decide to live a different kind of life than you have until now.

. . .

If you've been competing with others for years, it may feel impossible to imagine a future where you're not driven by the fear of losing your edge.

But if you can decide, swiftly and wholeheartedly, to stop striving for specialness, you may find yourself living more peacefully than ever, as if a weight has simply fallen off your shoulders. You'll wonder why you've struggled so much all this time, and you'll be able to relax, breathe and perform better at work.

To help you reach that point, this book encourages you to step away from all competition. 'But that's impossible!' you may object. 'Even if *I* stop, everyone else will keep competing!'

Perhaps. But no one stays undefeated forever. Even those who have long trusted in their ability to claim victory will face moments that shake their confidence.

For someone who has always excelled, it's extremely difficult to admit that they might be ordinary. It can feel like confessing to mediocrity.

But that's not what it means.

When people resist the idea of being ordinary, it's because the word carries a range of different meanings. The ordinary you reject – meaning *the same as everyone else* – isn't the same ordinary I'm talking about.

As we'll see, you absolutely *shouldn't* live your life as a copy of others. But you also don't need to be special to live differently.

. . .

Let's start with a simple but slippery question: what does it mean to be special – and why do so many of us feel we have to be?

The truth is, you don't need to be special at all. In practice, chasing distinction often makes life heavier, harsher and much more difficult to enjoy.

Even someone who has always been top of the class, has never lost a competition and feels destined for success can suddenly face a moment that rattles their confidence. And that moment – unwelcome as it is – can become the turning point of a lifetime.

If you've never doubted your own brilliance, then maybe you've also never felt that quiet dread: 'What if I'm actually ordinary?' However, accepting your own ordinariness is the first step towards putting down the emotional backpack you've been dragging around for years.

This book won't help you get your specialness back. So long as you're clinging to the idea that you have to be unique, real confidence will always slip through your fingers.

To be ordinary simply means accepting that you don't *need* to be special.

It means living as you are – different by nature, not by force. It's freedom from trying to look impressive, from competing non-stop, from grinding yourself down. It's the space where your real strengths are finally allowed to breathe.

My hope is that by the time you finish reading this book, you'll feel lighter – relaxed enough to go about your life with at least a little less friction.

# 1

# WHY DO I BELIEVE I HAVE TO BE SPECIAL?

## Why Comparisons Are a Trap

If you've ever had the sinking thought that maybe you're rather ordinary, then before that moment, you probably believed you were somehow different – maybe even exceptional. For people who grew up with great grades and constant praise, that realisation often comes later in life, which means it hits all the harder.

None of us *wants* to face experiences that knock our confidence off balance. But they happen – a disappointing exam score, or rejection from a university you were sure you would get into, for instance. In today's world, this can happen even earlier – failing to get into a school you worked hard for, or getting in and realising everyone around you is just as smart as you are, making you *unexceptional* by comparison. Anyone would lose their confidence in such a situation.

I saw this firsthand during my time teaching Ancient Greek at a university – the language Plato and Aristotle spoke in fourth- and fifth-century BCE Athens. My students were outstanding; they could read English, German, French and even some Latin with ease.

But once, a student who had probably never struggled with anything found themselves unable to translate a basic Greek exercise. They lowered their head, and flat-out refused to try. That may well have been their first time thinking, *Maybe I'm not special, after all.*

I understood them well. I started teaching Greek after majoring in the history of Western philosophy during my own student days. I thought my Greek was pretty good when I joined my research lab – until I met older students who could read it like a modern language. Then, newer students arrived, and they quickly caught up, too. Watching them handle texts I struggled with made me think, *Perhaps I'm not actually so exceptional.*

Some of my own students, too, looked shaken when they discovered they couldn't translate Greek while others could.

There's nowhere to hide when you're studying a foreign language. Your mistakes show instantly. It's humbling – and sometimes, it's crushing. But of course, it takes time to read original texts, which means there's nothing to do *but* study.

It surprised me to see students who had always believed they were good at languages fall silent in frustration at the realisation that they were just like everyone else, but still, I understood them. I, too, had gone through the trial of learning that I might not be as gifted as I had thought.

Gaining confidence as a capable scholar is extremely difficult, as is true in any discipline, and only the highly exceptional stand out. If you only look within your own country, you end up like the proverbial frog in a well that knows nothing of the ocean. My own field of study is filled with researchers from all over the world. Unlike when I was a student, the internet today opens us up with instant access to the work of researchers worldwide. Faced with such a vast pool of peers, it's easy for even those who consider themselves talented to lose confidence.

Work shows results in numbers, too. For instance, when I write books, and I worry about sales after publication. No matter how much time and energy I put into a book, if it doesn't sell immediately, I end up doubting my own ability.

Confidence built on being special is surprisingly fragile.

But numbers alone don't reveal the real value of a book, of course. There are a great many kinds of work that can't be measured quantitatively. Most people would agree that you can't judge the value of an artwork with points, for example, and the same goes for literature. Even in academics, poor exam results don't prove someone lacks ability.

When I was in middle school, I once glanced at a classmate's drawing and, thinking mine was terrible in comparison, started over from scratch. I can't remember if I ever finished that drawing. Today, I no longer believe one quick glimpse is enough to judge the quality of someone's art. And even if I had produced something similar to my classmate, it would no longer have been truly my own work.

Be it a book or a painting, you can't immediately discern its value. As such, it makes no sense to judge your own worth by casually comparing your work with someone else's.

People who believe that high sales equal high value will think their book or product is worthless if it doesn't sell. But such people fail to recognise the unique value in their own work – or in anyone else's, for that matter; they fail to see that true worth can't be measured by quantitative standards.

The simple fact of the matter is that comparing your work to someone else's is pointless.

## The Day I Stopped Trying to Be Special

The realisation that I wasn't special didn't dawn on me all at once. For me, the first hint at my own ordinariness came early, though it wouldn't come to a head until much later.

'You're smart – you should go to Kyoto University,' my grandfather would often say to me. Because of that, I *believed* I was smart.

This was before I even entered primary school, so my understanding was vague – I simply thought that going to Kyoto University was something adults would praise me for. I doubt I understood the real meaning behind my grandfather's words.

I didn't know what *being smart* actually meant, nor did I know what he saw in me that made him say it. Since this was before school, he obviously wasn't judging my ability based on test scores. Sometimes, adults say a child is smart merely because they develop language early – perhaps that was all he meant.

Nevertheless, I grew up believing I was smart. But when I received my first school report, my result in maths was a three out of five. I looked at that grade and thought, *Well, so much for Kyoto University.*

It was the day before summer break. On the way home, I kept taking the report out of my backpack, unable to stop staring at it. That day, looking at that card, I thought, *I'm not special. I'm just average.*

Yet even then, I still couldn't stop *trying* to be special.

As an adult, I originally studied philosophy, but later, I discovered the field of individual psychology, founded by the Austrian psychiatrist Alfred Adler. In many regions, including Japan, it's also known as Adlerian psychology. The day I first attended a lecture on Adlerian psychology was a major turning point in my life. I've been studying it ever since.

When Oscar Christensen – a pupil of Rudolf Dreikurs, Adler's disciple – came to Japan to give a lecture in Osaka, I was eager to attend. The fee, however, was too high for a student of my means. When I told the organisers I couldn't afford it, they said I could get in for free if I interpreted. That was my way in, though, in the end, my mentor handled all the interpreting during the lecture.

Feeling awkward, I sat and listened. When the Q&A session began, I asked a question. Since I hadn't been able to interpret, I at least wanted to ask it in English. But instead of answering, Christensen began telling a story:

'I remember one day, we were assigned a paper asking us to compare Adlerian psychology with another form of psychology in two pages. I wrote ten. The day after I submitted my report, my professor called me in.'

*Who writes ten pages when two will do?* I wondered.

Christensen continued: 'My professor asked me, "Why did you write so much?" "Because I was interested in the comparison," I answered. "No," he said. "That's not it. You wanted to impress me. But you're already good enough as you are. You don't need to do that." Until then, I had always tried to stand out. But after that incident, I learned to live like the youngest sibling.'

Living like the youngest sibling means you don't have to accomplish everything alone – you're allowed to ask for help when you need it.

At first, I thought his story was unrelated to my question. But it wasn't long before I realised his anecdote was directed at me.

I hadn't asked my question in English because my English was strong. I had done so to impress Christensen and everyone else in the room – to show them that I was capable. Christensen wasn't saying my English was *good enough*. He was saying I didn't need to try to set myself apart from everyone else. I didn't need to be unique. It was okay to be ordinary.

*That* was the day I stopped trying to be special.

## How Birth Order Shapes Our Lifestyle Choices

I was short as a child, and not very good at sports. I never stood out in class. Convinced that my height kept me from being recognised, I decided that at least academically, I would never lose to anyone. Kids who were good academically weren't necessarily popular, but studying was all I had.

There's no doubt that studying to avoid losing to others, or to gain approval, is an impure motive. But back then, I really did believe that I *had* to be special.

Not everyone starts out with this belief. But one early moment that makes you feel different can send you chasing that feeling for the rest of your life. More precisely, it becomes the moment you decide to strive for specialness.

Once you've set that goal, you choose a *character* to help you pursue it. One meaning of the word character is how you view the world, others and yourself. If you see the world as dangerous and other people as threats ready to harm you, that's one aspect of a character. If you see yourself as incompetent, that, too, becomes part of your character. Others take more positive views of the world and themselves.

How you deal with problems is also part of your character.

And people typically respond to problems in the same way every time.

Adler used the term *lifestyle*. The word character can sound innate and unchangeable, but Adler believed we each *choose* our lifestyle. Why? Because children born to the same parents and raised in the same environment can develop wildly different personalities. The only explanation is that they make different choices.

*But I don't remember* choosing *my character*, you might think. And that's fair. But if you *did* choose it, then you can change it – even as an adult. If character were innate and fixed, neither education nor rehabilitation would be possible.

That said, a lifestyle isn't chosen in a single moment or triggered by just one experience. Small children choose again and again, and at around age ten, they finally decide: 'This is the lifestyle I'll live by'. From then on, it rarely undergoes any dramatic changes.

Even though we say a lifestyle is something we choose ourselves, it's not as if we pick it freely out of thin air. Certain forces shape that choice. Parents' values and the culture a child grows up in matter, of course – but an even stronger influence is the child's relationship with their siblings. Birth order – whether you grow up as the firstborn, second-born, middle child, youngest or an only child – plays a major role in shaping your lifestyle.

· · ·

Central to how childhood shapes us is what Adler called *dethronement*.

Before a younger sibling is born, the firstborn enjoys their parents' complete attention, interest and affection. But once a new baby arrives, the parents must inevitably devote time and energy to them – even if they want to treat the older child exactly the same as before. Parents may not *intend* to spoil the newborn, but the shift in focus can feel unacceptable to the firstborn – especially if they grew up receiving excessive attention simply because they were the only child.

Parents ask the firstborn to understand that things have changed, but if the child can't grasp why their world is suddenly different, they feel that the time, focus and warmth they once monopolised have been stolen by the new baby. *That* is dethronement. To the firstborn, the younger sibling becomes a rival. And second-born children may face the same experience when another baby arrives after them.

Still, it's worth noting that not every child in the same situation feels dethroned. A stone dropped from your hand will always fall, but in his work *The Education of Children*, Adler described dethronement as a *psychological fall*, meaning it doesn't happen automatically. Some children believe they've fallen from the throne: others don't. It's not uncommon for a child to delight in the arrival of a sibling and try to help their parents. Many firstborns, however, feel displaced by a younger sibling, and try to reclaim the throne. To do that, they seek attention by trying to stand out.

They begin by trying to be *good*. When a parent says, 'You're the older brother/sister now,' and urges them to do things on their own, the firstborn tries to live up to those expectations. A child who once couldn't fall asleep without a parent might suddenly go to bed alone, or start helping with chores. They try to be *exceptionally* good – because they believe that unless they excel, their parents won't pay attention to them.

When they successfully complete a task their parents ask of them, they are praised. But children who are praised start striving to be good – not just good, but special – in order to get more praise, though praise isn't guaranteed. Worse, if they fail at a task, or try to help with the baby and accidentally make them cry, the parent may scold them.

They want to make their parents happy, yet they get chewed out. When this repeats, they may stop trying to be *good* and begin doing things that trouble their parents – having toilet accidents, crying at night or wetting the bed. Skills they used to manage easily become things they can't do anymore.

Some even develop more disruptive behaviours – often called *regression*. These behaviours exist for one purpose: to get attention. Children don't want to be scolded, but they deliberately create trouble at the moment their parents least want it to ensure they'll be noticed.

It isn't that the parents love the firstborn any less – they're simply overwhelmed caring for the new baby. But the firstborn can't grasp this. And when they get scolded, it only reinforces the belief that they aren't loved anymore – that they are no longer *special*.

. . .

The push to be special isn't limited to firstborns, of course. Second-born children also try to be special, though perhaps in a different way.

Everything is new for the firstborn. Entering primary school, then secondary school – every experience is a first for both child and parents. However, younger siblings grow up watching the firstborn, so they learn more efficiently and make fewer missteps. In this way, the firstborn acts like the pacemaker at the front of the race; if you run right behind the leader, you don't have to take the wind straight on. But brothers and sisters constantly compete with the firstborn, trying to catch up and overtake. The moment the firstborn shows the slightest weakness, the younger sibling seizes the chance to sprint ahead.

A second-born child may refuse to accept anyone else taking the lead. They believe that no authority is unbeatable and resist yielding to anyone's control. And especially when facing the firstborn, who sees themselves as an extension of parental authority, the second-born feels they must never lose to them.

When a younger child is born after the second-born, the second-born becomes the middle child, squeezed between siblings. Because an older sibling already existed when they were born, middle children never receive the full, undivided attention that firstborns enjoy. And when a younger sibling arrives, parental attention shifts once more, causing the middle child to feel, just as the firstborn did, that their parents' attention and affection have been taken away. It's less often the case that this actually happens than that the child *believes* it to be true.

Middle children often receive the least attention, and they may act out to get it. On the other hand, they sometimes become the most independent of all siblings. They learn early not to rely on their parents, and thus they may be the first to leave home for further education or work.

The youngest child never experiences dethronement. They're often the most indulged – the family's eternal baby. Even if the youngest can't do things their older siblings could at the same age, parents don't tend to worry too much.

As a result, youngest children can become dependent, asking their parents to do things they should handle themselves. Yet constant stimulation from older siblings can also push the youngest to develop quickly and even surpass them. Because they don't want to admit lagging behind older, more experienced siblings, the youngest may come to believe they *have* to be talented – that they have to find a way to be special – and that brings its own problems.

• • •

No matter where a child falls in the birth order, each one often tries to be special to win a parent's attention. They tell themselves, 'If I'm not special, no one will notice me.'

Yet not all children respond this way. Some don't care about standing out at all, and even as adults, plenty of people work hard without craving recognition. They simply don't see any value in attention in and of itself; for them, the value lies in the act of doing, not in being seen.

In my case, I wasn't one of them. As a young child, I wasn't recognised for all the studying I did. Being good at school didn't automatically make me stand out. Yet even so, once I started earning good grades, I shaped myself around that image – the kid who does well – and I started *trying* to be special. I was responding to what I *thought* others expected of me, without ever stopping to ask whether anyone had actually expected it in the first place.

## How Parental Approval Feeds
## the Desire to Be Special

Feeling ignored by a parent is, at least in most cases, just how the child perceives the situation. Parents usually try to treat each child equally, so they're often shocked when a child comes out with a remark like, 'You don't care about me anymore.' Yet if those same parents look back on their own childhoods, they may recall feeling less loved themselves once a younger sibling came along.

As we've covered, children compete for their parents' attention, concern and affection. In order to win that competition, they convince themselves they need to be exceptional. When it comes to studying, for instance, that translates into believing they have to get good grades.

While birth order certainly introduces competition among siblings in these ways, parental behaviour can amplify it, especially through praise and discipline.

When a child misbehaves, parents scold them. When a child behaves or does something the parent likes, they get their approval. Naturally, some children are praised often, and some almost never; some are scolded constantly, and others rarely.

Every child wants praise, but no one can behave perfectly all the time – and as we saw earlier, once that praise disappears, a child may act out to get attention (even negative attention).

Take drawing pictures. Drawing is fun and should be satisfying on its own. But a child who craves praise brings the drawing to the parent for approval. A parent might not bluntly say, 'That's terrible,' but if the child doesn't get the reaction they hoped for, disappointment sets in. Sometimes, they'll crumple up the drawing – even one they worked hard on – and throw it away.

This child didn't draw for joy. They drew to be praised, and so without that, the drawing has no value.

A great many people believe praise is essential in both parenting and education, but we need to understand its pitfalls. Studying to win a parent's approval and not studying to upset a parent are two sides of the same coin: they're both attempts to be special by manipulating a parent's attention.

Adler said this about praise, in the context of children who have been told they are very promising:

> So long as they are helped and appreciated, they can go forward; but when the time comes to make independent efforts, their courage fails, and they retreat.
>
> (*What Life Should Mean to You*)

Adler sometimes sounded as if he supported praise, but here he speaks plainly about its dangers. A 'pampered' child moves forward as long as they are supported and applauded, but when it's time to rely on themselves, they can lose courage and pull back.

A child who grows up thinking they must be special, outshining their siblings to win their parents' attention, will eventually study and work for the same reason: to earn approval.

Some argue that praise helps people grow, but the same problem shows up with a manager and an employee: praise makes people eager when they get it, but when it dries up, their motivation can shrivel up with it.

# The Influence of Parental Values

The values a family holds dear can shape a child's entire life. If those values are so strong that a child must either accept them or fight against them, they inevitably have a profound effect on the choices the child makes about their lifestyle.

Academic credentials are a prime example. If both parents are convinced that schooling is essential, or if even just one parent is and the topic sparks constant arguments, then the weight of those values becomes enormous.

Parents who believe academic achievement is crucial scold a child with poor grades, or at least grow visibly sour. On the flip side, they praise good grades. Naturally, a child who longs for that praise throws themselves into studying, trying hard to bring home good results so they can be special in their parents' eyes.

If the parents are highly educated, the child often aims for the same path as them. But some children announce that they don't want to pursue education and want to start working as soon as they can. A lot of parents push back. When a child chooses a path completely different from the one their parents lived, parental anxiety can skyrocket.

When a child decides to live a different life in order to rebel, they're still caught in their parents' value system. The life you choose must be your own, independent of parental values. If you choose something merely to oppose your parents, you're still not living your own life.

On the other hand, a child who follows their parents' values when choosing a path is still trying to win approval and probably trying to outshine their siblings. But again, the choice isn't their own – they are guided by those parental values. Children like this aim to live the kind of life most people live. And it's not just to please their parents. They're afraid of living in a way their parents wouldn't recognise; afraid of stepping outside the boundaries of what's considered normal.

## How the 'Special' Mindset Becomes Fixed

A child raised to compete with siblings and to believe they must be special – shaped heavily by parental values – keeps doing the same thing later, only with different people. At school and then in society, the pattern repeats.

As they grow older, striving to be unique makes them increasingly self-conscious about how others see them. They begin moulding themselves to the image they think others expect of them. In school, they protect their sense of uniqueness by playing a role: the smart one, the athlete, the popular kid.

And this mindset – *I have to be special* – continues straight into adulthood.

# 2

# THE FRAGILE SUPERIORITY OF THOSE WHO NEED TO BE SPECIAL

## People Who Are Habitually Tense

Someone who studies hard, gets top grades, sails into their dream university and seems to be cruising through life still can't stay outstanding forever.

Yes, there are people who keep producing great results for an extended period, but even they don't necessarily possess unshakeable confidence. However, if you asked someone who looks confident whether they secretly suspect they can't stay exceptional forever, they would probably deny it on the spot.

If you've already gone through an experience that shook your confidence, I would urge you to see it as a turning point — an invitation to live the rest of your life differently. Letting go of the belief that you have to be special can change everything.

That being said, challenging the assumptions you've held your whole life is no easy task.

You'll continue to study and work hard. I'm not saying effort is optional. But you *do* need to stop wasting your energy on the wrong goal — on trying to be special.

Adler often cited cases of what he called *habitually tense* people. These are the people who believe they *have* to be extraordinary.

There's a case study in Adler's *The Science of Living* about a man suffering from insomnia, who had been largely ignored as a child. One day, when his usual form teacher was absent, a substitute stepped in, saw his potential and encouraged him, likely offering up a few words of encouragement – phrases like, 'You can do this.' From that moment on, he suddenly began earning high marks, but he still couldn't bring himself to *believe* he was capable. Yet he felt constantly pushed from behind, studying all day and into the evening. As an adult, he convinced himself that the only way to accomplish anything was to stay active most of the night, leading to insomnia.

According to Adler, people like this are 'habitually tense' and hold deep anxieties about their ability to succeed.

Those who strive to be special often resemble this man; they can't fully believe in their own skills and are always wound up tight about producing good results.

I myself studied relentlessly when I was a student, yet I never felt genuinely capable. Even after finishing school, that feeling lingered for years. I kept telling myself that while I didn't have the kind of talent that made everything come easily, effort itself was a kind of talent – and for me, that would have to be enough.

It's true that accomplishment demands effort, and I certainly worked harder than most. But looking back, I suspect I fit Adler's description of the habitually tense.

# People Who Feel Crushed
# by Others' Expectations

Adler also described a nine-year-old girl who tired easily and complained of headaches. She loved school and studied far more than necessary, but Adler explained this as a sign of insecurity.

> *She longs to accomplish something big, but believes she can do so only through extreme effort.*
>
> (*Individual Psychology in the School*)

This girl's excessive effort wasn't just about insecurity; there was something more important driving her.

> *She works excessively hard to please, especially her teacher.*

As Adler wrote 'especially her teacher', it's clear the girl wasn't trying to please *only* the teacher. She must have wanted to please her parents as well, to avoid disappointing the people who believed in her.

The man with insomnia in the previous section also earned good grades, but his drive to study so intensely likely came from wanting to please the teacher who had noticed his talent.

*He carries the constant burden of others' expectations, pushed forward at every moment, and is overly preoccupied with himself.*

(The Science of Living)

This pressure arises from trying to cover up what Adler called a 'superiority complex that merely pretends at excellence'.

A superiority complex is the urge to show off one's supposed superiority. People with this complex inflate their image because deep down, they suspect they're not actually exceptional. A superiority complex is always rooted in a feeling of inferiority. That's what Adler meant by 'pretends at excellence'.

Here, Adler points to another problem with habitual tension: people who feel crushed by expectations are actually preoccupied with how others see them.

Think of an Olympic athlete who believes they're carrying a nation on their shoulders. Sometimes, the weight of expectation keeps them from performing at their best. Families, coaches and fans want a medal; the athlete feels they must deliver, and if they can't, they fear they won't be able to face the public.

Adler said that those who feel this burden of expectation are, paradoxically, focused entirely on themselves – because their attention is fixed on how they appear to others.

*Children who have been heavily burdened with expectations begin to falter in their studies or work,*

*while those who once seemed less capable catch up and
reveal unexpected abilities.*

(*What Life Should Mean to You*)

This describes how trying too hard to meet expectations can
sabotage performance. A gold-medal favourite might unexpect-
edly lose in the first round, while an underdog shines. The failure
isn't because the task is beyond them – they might have more
than enough ability – but because the pressure itself derails them.

*When they test their own strength, they feel as though
standing at the edge of an abyss, and shocked by the
fear that their lack of worth will be exposed, they begin to
retreat.*

(*Social Interest: A Challenge to Mankind*)

If someone simply lacks the necessary skill, they can usually
study more and improve. Or, if they're an athlete, they can train
harder. But Adler said that when they fear their lack of worth
will be revealed, they start to pull back.

Adler's use of the word *worth* needs explanation. He also
wrote:

*You can have courage only when you feel that you
have worth.*

(*Adler Speaks: The Lectures of Alfred Adler*)

In the context of study or work, worth includes both ability
and the expectations a person believes others have placed on them.

35

*They worry that they may betray the expectations that have been placed on them.*

*(What Life Should Mean to You)*

Someone with a superiority complex, who's fixated on how they appear to others, assumes parents or teachers expect great things, and believes they must deliver. If they can't earn high marks, or if they sense that they're falling short, their craving for approval can become so strong that they resort to dishonesty.

When a brilliant academic plagiarises, for example, it's often because they believe that they'll let people down if they don't remain exceptional – even though, in reality, it's possible that no one is expecting all that much.

## The Inferiority Behind the Need to Be Special

Children who work hard to meet the expectations of others grow into adults who work much the same way – pushing themselves too hard and always feeling habitually tense.

> *The habitual tension such people suffer is a sign that they doubt their ability to succeed, and that doubt is masked by a superiority complex that is, in fact, only a pretence of superiority.*

(*The Science of Living*)

They want to believe that their effort proves they are superior. But the reason they're pretending to be superior, as we've seen, is that they secretly believe they're not. A superiority complex is just a feeling of inferiority turned inside out. Adler put it like this:

> *It's as though they're standing on tiptoe to make themselves look bigger, hoping to gain success and superiority through some simple trick.*

(*The Science of Living*)

Adler isn't saying that puffing yourself up makes you superior. He's saying that some people believe it will – that they think projecting largeness is enough to secure success and superiority.

Of course, standing on tiptoe isn't what makes you truly great.

## Special People Who Eventually Stumble

In *The Science of Living*, Adler described cases of people who believe they are destined for a higher purpose. It may sound dramatic, but this simply means that someone sees themselves as different from everyone else – marked for greatness, set apart to accomplish something out of the ordinary.

Once, a man was on his way to a theatre in Vienna. By chance, an errand came up beforehand, so he took a detour to take care of it. When he finally arrived at the theatre, he found the entire building had burned to the ground.

Everything was gone, yet he had survived. It's easy to see how someone who lives through an experience like that might start to see themselves as special.

The problem comes later, when life hands them another experience that contradicts the expectation and promise they derived from that moment. When this man's marriage fell apart, he suffered a tremendous breakdown. His courage failed, he lost his emotional anchor and he slipped into depression.

This kind of setback isn't limited to relationships. People who have convinced themselves that they're unlike everyone else can be undone by something as trivial as a minor stumble at work. Their confidence is fragile.

## People Who Want to Be Seen as
## Special Yet Do Nothing

Adler wrote this about those who carry a sense of superiority:

> *There are people who feel they can accomplish anything.*
> *They believe they already know everything and see*
> *no need to learn. The result of this attitude is obvious:*
> *children who feel this way usually perform poorly in*
> *school.*

> (*The Science of Living*)

Adler also said that 'anyone can accomplish anything' – a point I'll return to in Chapter 4. What matters here is that he's criticising those who merely *feel* they can accomplish anything. They believe they could do it if they tried – yet they never actually try.

People who think they could do it if they wanted to are the ones who do nothing. Those who think they know everything are the ones who refuse to learn. Since they already see themselves as superior, they assume that learning is for the ignorant.

Some complain that what they learned in university is useless. Yet even if the content of your studies doesn't apply practically to real life, the research skills and writing habits you build when working on papers remain valuable long after you graduate. And because situations will always arise that demand knowledge you didn't already have, learning has to persist.

But people with a superiority complex refuse to learn anything new. It's not that they don't want to learn because they already know everything – they avoid learning because they don't want to face the possibility that they might try something new and fall short. They use their supposed superiority as justification for avoiding the risk of failure.

They insist they don't need to learn, but what they're really doing is sidestepping the possibility of not getting the results they expect.

They are sidestepping the possibility of discovering they are, in fact, ordinary.

# 3

# WHAT IT MEANS TO BE ORDINARY

## Why You Don't Need to Be Special

Having read this far, you might realise how much of your life you've spent believing you had to be special. Perhaps you weren't simply hardworking – maybe you were constantly worried about how others saw you, trying to meet expectations, trying to make yourself look more impressive than you actually felt. If that sounds familiar, then here's the truth: you don't have to do any of that. It is perfectly fine to just be ordinary.

Being ordinary means not fretting over other people's opinions and not trying to inflate your own image. Even saying *don't make yourself look more impressive than you are* already assumes an audience, but this isn't about them. It's about accepting yourself.

When people hear the word ordinary, they often imagine being stuck in the middle of some hierarchy, or being the same as those around them. They tie it to comparisons and rankings. They start to believe that accepting ordinariness is the same as admitting defeat. But none of this is about other people.

You don't need to chase praise to earn someone's attention, affection or love. You don't need to act out just to get noticed. You don't need to be exceptionally good or exceptionally bad.

Whether in your studies or in your job, you don't have to be special to be recognised. Showing up as you are is enough.

Trying to appear better than you are is vanity. Someone who pretends to know everything is far less admirable than someone who acknowledges what they don't know and carries on. In school, at work, everywhere you go, that kind of straightforward honesty ends up earning a lot more respect.

. . .

People who have spent their lives trying to be special often recoil from the word ordinary.

If you believed you had to stand out and spent years competing with others, then ordinary very well might sound like being lumped together with everyone else. And being lumped together feels like stepping out of the contest – or even losing. So, when you hear the word ordinary, you may assume it's synonymous with sameness, conformity or surrender.

In this chapter, I want to unravel that assumption and explore what ordinary means – to show you that you don't need to be special, but at the same time, you don't have to blend into the crowd.

## Ordinary Doesn't Mean Boring

Being ordinary does *not* mean being identical to everyone else. And you don't have to become special in order to justify being different.

If being ordinary truly meant being exactly the same as the people around you, then it would be natural to avoid it. However, take job hunting, for example. In Japan, most people wear similar suits while interviewing – and that's okay. What actually matters isn't the surface-level conformity, which merely demonstrates your awareness of what's appropriate and expected in the situation – it's how clearly you communicate your own values and perspective.

You don't engage in some performance of superiority. Speaking plainly about your experiences and motivations naturally conveys who you are. You don't get hired by trying to be exceptional. You get hired by being honest about how you want to contribute and what kind of work you want to do.

Job hunting looks like a competition, but in reality, it's a process of confirming mutual fit. Sure, sometimes you realise the company isn't right for you. But you don't need to posture or try to stand out loudly. When you leave all pretensions at the door, you're far more likely to be recognised as a distinct individual.

Let go of the idea that you have to be special. Stop forcing differentiation. Show up as yourself – *that's* what it means to be ordinary.

## When It's Tempting to Follow the Crowd

People who try to come across as special while job hunting often carry a deep preoccupation with how others see them. It may seem counterintuitive at first, but those same people stop speaking up once they're hired. Under a nebulous pressure to conform, they bottle up their opinions and suppress what they really think.

When I was in high school, I used to ask teachers all sorts of questions during class. My classmates, however, didn't appreciate it when I did this close to the end of a lesson, as my questions cut into their break time. Still, I asked whenever I didn't understand something. And of course, the teacher would answer – that's what teaching is. None the less, I could feel the pressure from classmates telling me, 'Just stop it already,' and it was always tempting to remain silent and not stand out.

A similar desire to remain inconspicuous sometimes happens in the workplace. You may notice that your boss – or the company itself – is doing something questionable. If no one speaks up, the surface stays calm. But sometimes, employees get hurt, or the company earns money by doing socially harmful work. Sometimes, supervisors engage in outright misconduct. If you pay attention, you'll see more of this than you might expect.

Yet plenty of people stay silent because they don't want to stand out or be targeted. Watching whistleblowers suffer the consequences of speaking up only reinforces that fear. Sometimes, however, it's not that people stay silent to avoid standing out – they go along with everyone else because they feel they *have* to. For example, when a boss tells their staff to attend a boozy party or some awful-sounding company event, you may reluctantly fall in line because everyone else is going, and you don't want to be the only one who declines.

People who give in to peer pressure, even though they believe they shouldn't stay silent, still have their own views. But those who decide from the outset to do exactly what everyone else does may not even recognise that what's happening around them is unreasonable. They may feel no inner conflict at all – not even the frustration of knowing they should speak up but can't.

If you've always earned good grades since your student days, you probably don't worry much about standing out. You may even try to highlight your competence and distinguish yourself. Yet even people like this fall silent once they realise that speaking up could hurt their chances of promotion.

The philosopher Kiyoshi Miki put it this way:

*The quickest way to control subordinates is to instil in them the ideology of advancement and success.*

(Notes on the Theory of Life)

Young people today may not be particularly driven by dreams of climbing the ladder, but when your livelihood is effectively being held hostage, you naturally fear rocking the boat by upsetting the atmosphere at work. For a boss, it's easy to control employees who prioritise self-preservation.

Still, if a superior says something unreasonable, you shouldn't just stay silent – even when no one else speaks up. Raising your voice may mean you can no longer blend in with the crowd, but what matters in life is being able to decide for yourself what should be done and to act accordingly, without giving in to the pressure to conform.

# Society Needs People Who Speak Up

From the perspective of the organisation as a whole, any group where everyone thinks the same way and does the same things, or where thinking differently isn't welcomed, will never develop. Original work simply doesn't emerge in such environments.

In workplaces, for example, supervisors have a responsibility to teach those who come after them, but it's not enough for junior staff to simply accept everything a boss says. No matter how capable a superior may be, they're not always right. That's why junior staff must think for themselves, ask questions when necessary and voice their opinions. Even the most long-standing of customs sometimes needs to be revised to match changes in society and the times. Individual proposals may be rejected, but if no one ever speaks up, nothing will ever change.

If you think your workplace atmosphere doesn't allow people to speak their minds, you may simply be using that as an excuse for not asserting your own ideas. The first step to addressing this is to stop focusing on who said something and instead focus solely on what was said, and whether it's right or wrong.

All it takes is one person to start doing things differently for the atmosphere at work to begin to change. To make that happen, you need to concentrate on communicating your point accurately and stop worrying about how you might be perceived. If you stop fixating on how you're seen and trust that what you say will be judged on its substance, there is no need to be afraid.

In workplaces where people criticise speakers rather than ideas, no one wants to raise their hand. But when the focus shifts to examining the content of what is said, open discussion follows naturally.

Once you start paying attention to *who* is speaking, it becomes much harder to voice dissent. So when others speak, listen to the content alone, and if you disagree, simply offer them an alternative viewpoint.

Practically speaking, when you disagree with someone, make it clear that you're opposing the statement, not the person.

First, you might clearly state whether you agree or disagree and explain your reasoning carefully. If you want to invite others into the discussion, don't direct your point back only to the original speaker. Instead, say something like, 'I'm opposed (or in favour) for these reasons … What do the rest of you think?' and open it up to the group.

At the same time, you mustn't speak up only for the sake of being *seen* as competent or special. Doing so shifts attention to the person speaking rather than what is being said. What matters isn't how you're perceived, but the wellbeing of others. For example, even if a company you are part of profits, if its actions harm the local community, the nation or the world, then regardless of how you yourself are viewed, you must ask whether that's really acceptable.

If people stop voicing dissent and fail to say what needs to be said, communities become closed. You don't need to be special in order to avoid being the same as everyone else. What's necessary is the ability to assert your own thinking.

Those who try to be the same and those who try to be special are ultimately both preoccupied with themselves – with how they're seen by others. In contrast, people who say what needs to be said without worrying about appearances are focusing not on others' evaluations, but on other people themselves.

There are times when people may not think well of you for speaking up. Yet even so, you can believe that asserting your view and correcting mistakes ultimately benefits others.

People who *want* to be special believe they have to be recognised. But even when you don't set out to be special, solid work earns recognition. Yes, work that's far ahead of its time may go unrecognised – but work done with the goal of being special or earning praise rarely turns out to be truly good work.

## You Don't Need to Stand Out to Be Different

Most people who insist on being better than others have lived since childhood in a state of constant competition. Competition feels so natural to them that they can't begin to imagine the world without it. And once you believe you *have* to win, life becomes a constant state of tension.

It's understandable not to want to be the same as everyone else, and as we've seen, there are times when you shouldn't be the same. But being different doesn't necessarily mean standing out.

You don't need to advertise how unique you are loudly just to avoid being seen as the same. Competence matters at work, and companies do hire capable people – but being conspicuous doesn't necessarily mean being capable.

Referring once again to *Adler Speaks: The Lectures of Alfred Adler*, he said, 'You can have courage only when you feel that you have worth.' In work, this means that when you believe you're competent, you gain the courage to engage fully with your tasks.

You *do* need the necessary knowledge and skills to be competent. But what matters most is actually *being* capable — not trying to *look* capable by emphasising how different you are.

Years ago, I gave a lecture at the main offices of a travel agency. It happened to be job-interview day, and a large number of young applicants were waiting outside the room. Among them was an individual wearing traditional ethnic clothing from a southeast Asian country. Surrounded by applicants in standard recruitment suits, this person stood out like a sore thumb.

I still remember someone from the company saying, 'There's no way that person will pass.' At the time, I wondered whether the company simply wanted people who would unquestioningly do as they were told, but looking back, it's more likely they saw through the fragility of someone who overemphasises being different — and the emptiness of trying to stand out for its own sake.

Few people try something so unusual in an interview, and even if they do, it tells you nothing about whether they can do the job. The same applies to someone who believes they have to be special at work. They're no different from the person who showed up to an interview in conspicuous clothing. At work, what matters is delivering results. To do that, you simply have to put in the effort — you don't need to work for recognition.

Furthermore, *results* don't only mean outcomes that show up clearly in numbers. If a company fails to value contributions that can't be quantified, then being told you're not capable simply because you don't produce visible numbers doesn't actually mean you lack ability. It may just mean your contributions aren't being properly acknowledged.

# Choose a Life That's Truly Your Own

In this book, *ordinary* doesn't mean doing the same things as everyone else. In fact, this chapter has shown many situations where thinking and acting like everyone else is precisely what you *shouldn't* do.

The same is true when it comes to how you live your life in general. You don't need to model yourself on everyone else − and in fact, you shouldn't. Yet many people try to do exactly that.

Why? Because they've never really thought about how *they* want to live.

Parental influence plays a major role here. Many parents want their children to be exceptional, pushing them to study from a young age. Children burdened with high parental ideals work hard to meet those expectations, but while the life that grows out of such effort may *look* special, in reality, it often differs little from the lives of countless others.

Children are shaped by their parents and try to live the lives their parents expect. But even so, the choice is theirs. If you choose to live exactly as your parents tell you to, you end up living *their* lives, not your own.

The same applies to those who model themselves on the majority. They, too, fail to chart their own course. You may think no one truly *avoids* living for themselves – but some people do. Put simply, they don't want to take responsibility for their choices.

Such people believe that if they live the life their parents prescribed for them, or a life just like everyone else's, then when things go wrong, they won't have to see it as their own personal failure. Of course, when things do go wrong, no one actually takes responsibility for them – but they lack the confidence to decide for themselves how to live.

Even the drive to be special often isn't a choice made freely. It's something people internalise under the influence of parental and societal expectations.

This takes us back to the question that underpins the whole book: how can you stop believing you have to be special, and instead develop the courage to be ordinary? To answer this, we need to focus on any underlying feelings of inferiority you may have and how to overcome them – which is exactly what we'll do in Chapter 4.

# 4

# OVERCOMING FEELINGS OF INFERIORITY

# The Illusion of Cause and Effect

When a co-worker or a junior colleague delivers better results than you do, you might find yourself thinking, *I'm more capable – I have a better academic background*, or contrastingly, *I thought I was special, but maybe I'm actually pretty ordinary*. Even then, some people refuse to accept what's right in front of them: the reality that the other person's actions were what caused the outcome. It was never anything to do with who you are.

Those who cling tightly to academic credentials often seem to be habitually tense types (see p. 31) – people who, deep down, don't truly believe in their own excellence. Call it an inferiority complex and many will push back, but the truth is that this sense of inferiority acts like a brake when you're trying to do your job. Take your foot off that brake, and you can produce far better results than you are right now.

Whether things go poorly or well, it's common to look for causes in places that, in reality, have nothing to do with the outcome. For this, Adler used the term 'the illusion of cause and effect' (*Social Interest: A Challenge to Mankind*). What he meant is that people often want to believe there's a causal relationship between things, where none actually exists.

## There Is No Causal Relationship Between Education and Ability

Academic background is an indicator of ability, but believing there's a causal relationship between education and ability is a classic example of this illusion of cause and effect. People who think this way often study relentlessly from childhood, aiming for a prestigious university. They believe that getting into a famous school will make others see them as capable.

It's rare for a child to decide they want to attend an elite secondary school completely of their own volition. What drives that decision is usually a parent who believes, 'To succeed in the future, you have to get into a top university, and to do that, you should attend a top-notch school.' With that thought imparted to them by their parents, the child studies for entrance exams, gets into university and comes to believe that their academic record is proof of their competence.

But even if academic background is one indicator of ability, there's no causal relationship between graduating from a university and being truly capable. Some might argue that academic credentials at least prove a link between effort and ability. Yet, getting into a competitive university only shows that you worked hard *in the past*.

It's hard to find any causal connection between past effort – represented by academic credentials – and your ability to perform well at work now. Even if your degree reflects your ability at the time you graduated, it says nothing about whether you've continued to put in the effort since then.

It's also questionable whether passing a difficult exam truly proves competence in more general terms. Exams are popularly thought to be objective measures of ability, but failing to score well doesn't mean you lack skill, and scoring highly doesn't automatically mean you're capable. Judging ability based on a single exam – or even many – is notoriously unreliable. Even truly capable people won't ace a test every time.

There's a reason some people want to believe there's a causal link between education and ability. When they fail to produce good results, they want to think, *If only I'd graduated from a better university, I would have succeeded.* They pin the cause on an academic background they can no longer change, choosing to live in the realm of what might have been.

Others, when they don't get good results, may think, *I graduated from a good school, so I'm definitely capable – this failure must be a fluke. I just had bad luck.* They refuse to accept reality as it is. But again, this supposed link between education and ability is a baseless belief.

## Academic Background Is Just an Attribute

Academic background is nothing more than an attribute. An attribute is something like the smartness implied when you say, 'That person is smart.' Literally speaking, it's something that belongs to a person – it isn't the person themselves. Take off a hat, put on a different one, and you're still the same person. The university you graduated from is just one of your attributes.

Attributes are general by nature, and many people share the same ones. Individuality, on the other hand, can't be fully explained by attributes alone. Trying to fit yourself into the attribute of academic background essentially means erasing your own individuality. It's no different from young job seekers trying to mould themselves into the kind of ideal candidate a company claims to want.

Consider people who lean on the prestige of their alma mater rather than on themselves, telling others where they studied in order to place themselves inside the category of graduates from that university. Why do they feel the need to do this? Because they lack confidence. They believe they'll only be acknowledged through the attribute of academic credentials.

Some people introduce themselves on first meeting as if they're reading aloud from a résumé. When I meet someone like that, I want to tell them that I'm not interested in their academic or work history. They may hope I'll be impressed, but if I'm indifferent, they'll be disappointed. And even if those credentials carry weight at home, the name of their university might mean nothing at all abroad.

# 'Anyone Can Accomplish Anything'

If you stop believing there's a causal relationship between education and ability, then when you don't get good results at work, you can simply tell yourself, 'I went about it in the wrong way.' From there, you can approach the task differently next time. But if you believe that only capable or highly educated people can succeed, you'll never feel motivated to try a new approach.

We've already seen Adler's claim that 'anyone can accomplish anything' (*The Science of Living*). When he first made this argument, critics accused him of ignoring genetic differences. Adler went so far as to say, 'Belief in the inheritance of ability is probably the single greatest mistake ever made in the field of education' (*The Education of Children*).

What Adler wanted to highlight was the fact that many children decide from the outset not to tackle a challenge – not because they lack ability or because the task is too hard, but because they've given up before starting.

At the core of Adler's argument is this: if you assume from the beginning that you can't do something, that belief can become a lifelong fixed idea. Remove that assumption, and anyone can do anything. Thinking *I can't* trips you up at the starting line of every challenge you face.

This principle is democratic in the sense that it applies to everyone – not just those seen as capable – meaning that with effort, anyone can achieve anything. That's precisely why people who want to see themselves as especially gifted may resist it – it threatens the sense of superiority they cling so hard to.

There's a story about Adler's daughter, Alexandra, who later became a psychiatrist. As a child, she was bad at maths, and she once came home having skipped an exam. Her father said to her, 'What's going on? Do you really think you can't do something so ridiculously simple? Everyone else can do it. If you set your mind to it, you can, too.' Shortly after that, Alexandra became the top student in the class for maths (*Alfred Adler: As We Remember Him*).

You don't need to be number one, but with a little study, problems that once seemed impossible can become solvable. Alexandra didn't skip the exam because she was bad at maths. She did so because she thought that if she didn't take it, she wouldn't be evaluated at all. Of course, skipping the exam meant a zero, so that reasoning made no sense. But she preferred to think, *If I had taken it, I would have scored high*, rather than actually taking it and receiving a poor grade.

· · ·

People who skip an exam so they won't have to produce results, or who tell themselves, *If I'd taken the test, I would have scored well*, or, *If only I'd tried harder, I could have pulled it of* are living in the realm of possibility.

Some may argue that you can't necessarily accomplish everything, that no matter how hard you try, there are some things you simply can't do. But ask yourself this: aren't you sometimes ruling yourself out before you even start, deciding from the outset that you can't do it and therefore never taking on the challenge?

With effort and an informed approach, you can usually produce good results. Yet people who fear they might fail often hesitate before they even begin, or back off before they've put in real effort. In truth, this hesitation is just another way of avoiding the task itself. Even if you don't get great results right away, steady effort will build your ability little by little. If you tackle a challenge with the same determination you once brought to studying for your entrance exams, you can usually accomplish more than you believe, even when you're trying something entirely new.

## Inferiority Feelings Stand in the Way of Action

Those who have always thought of themselves as special have likely earned good grades and achieved success at work. They may believe they've never stood in their own way.

Still, when doubts creep in about whether you can maintain your track record, or experiences arise that make you wonder whether you might not be so special after all, those thoughts can easily become a roadblock when it's time to tackle a task.

People who strive to be special often work excessively hard, yet somewhere inside, they carry a sense of inferiority. That feeling acts as an anchor when they approach their work: putting in more effort while harbouring a sense of inferiority is like revving the engine while the anchor holds the boat in place.

There are always challenges in life that can't be avoided. One of them is work. For school pupils and university students, it's studying. As we saw earlier, Adler put it this way:

*You can have courage only when you feel that you have worth.*

(*Adler Speaks: The Lectures of Alfred Adler*)

Why does studying or working require courage? Because when you work, you produce results, and those results are evaluated. Even if the assessment is low, people who still believe they have value – who see themselves as capable – will keep taking on the challenge. Others, however, are frightened by the possibility of such evaluations and shrink back when faced with their work. About people like this, Adler said:

> *When they test their own strength, they feel as though standing at the edge of an abyss, and shocked by the fear that their lack of worth will be exposed, they begin to retreat.*
>
> (Social Interest: A Challenge to Mankind)

No job is accomplished effortlessly. Completing anything substantial requires effort. But people don't retreat because the task is objectively too difficult to complete. The real reason they feel that shock at the edge of the abyss is fear: the fear that their lack of worth will be exposed.

Those who believe they aren't capable, or who once thought they were capable but now doubt themselves, fear producing poor results and being negatively evaluated. Therefore, they avoid work altogether, or at least stop engaging with it proactively.

Even as their confidence in their own capability wavers, people who still want to believe they are competent and superior need a reason not to give their all. Deep down, they question themselves: 'What if I can't get good results? What if I'm not actually capable?' These are inferiority feelings. And having them provides, at the very least, a reason not to commit fully.

Ultimately, they're a form of self-defence: 'If I don't take on the task, I won't have to face the reality that I'm not capable.'

It's not that they truly lack ability and therefore can't work. While a lack of ability *is* inferiority, an inferiority feeling is simply that – a *feeling* of inferiority. It doesn't mean they actually are inferior. If they take on the work, they'll get results, and if they don't, they won't. But in order to avoid engaging with a problem, they first need a reason to back away, which is where those inferiority feelings come into play.

· · ·

Children don't start out believing they can't study. But when parents or teachers repeatedly tell a child with poor grades that they're *bad* at studying, the child begins to use a lack of ability as a reason not to engage with the task.

The same is true for people who once believed they were capable but then began to think they might not be. After just one failure, they assume they won't be able to find success again, and they stop challenging themselves. Because they've never been told they're bad at something they see as important, the setback shakes their confidence, and now they're tripping their own stride.

Adler said that because inferiority feelings are a form of weakness, people try to hide them. They are generally seen as evidence of failure – something shameful – so there's a strong tendency to conceal them. But by changing how you think about inferiority feelings, you can also change how you view your own abilities.

# Self-manufactured Anxiety Boxes You In

Creating inferiority feelings in order to avoid producing results at work stems from an anxiety about one's own abilities. But fear of results isn't the only reason people avoid tackling challenges.

Sometimes, you convince yourself that someone else is far more capable than you. You tell yourself that you could never compete, and so you avoid attempting the task altogether. Even if there's no rival right now, you worry that such a person might appear someday, and that anxiety makes you hesitate. Lacking confidence in your own abilities, you use the existence – or perhaps the imagined existence – of someone more capable to justify not taking action.

Even people who once thought of themselves as competent can become excessively anxious, thinking, *Maybe I'm just ordinary. Maybe I won't be able to achieve the same success as before.* That anxiety becomes a self-imposed ceiling. What matters here is that it's irrelevant whether a truly superior rival actually exists. All you need is the belief that there's someone more capable than you, someone you couldn't possibly compete against, to justify your decision not to engage. That person doesn't even have to be real.

. . .

The truth is that the only way to get through the challenge in front of you is to put in the effort, and not to allow your own manufactured anxiety to become the basis for an excuse. It is this thinking, rather than trying and producing disappointing results, that holds you back.

## Comparing Yourself Now to Your
## Past Self Stalls Growth

There are other triggers for anxiety as well. Younger people may find this difficult to imagine, but as you get older, you may start to feel that you no longer possess the memory or concentration you once did. You might still be capable at work, yet every now and then, you suddenly find yourself worrying about how long that will last. You remember how, when you were younger, you picked new skills up in no time at all, but now, you feel you just can't remember things the way you used to.

Even so, people who blame weaker results on declining memory, focus or stamina could still produce good outcomes if they tackled their work with the same discipline they once brought to the things they excelled at in the past. The real issue is that they've already decided not to engage fully, and so they don't even try to push themselves.

Even those who don't feel any obvious decline in their abilities sometimes compare their past selves with the person they are now and conclude that, whether it's work or learning something new, they can't perform as they once did. People like this avoid taking on new challenges and decide not to work as hard, stopping themselves before they can get off the ground. By doing so, they avoid disappointing results and can continue believing they're still capable as they once were.

Whether they would actually end up with disappointing results is beside the point. Just as with inferiority feelings or the imagined presence of rivals, they compare their past selves to their present selves and use the belief that they can no longer achieve the same results as a reason not to take on the task.

Some people who succeeded at work when they were young remain trapped by that success forever. They feel compelled to remind everyone of their past accomplishments – 'I was the one who edited that bestselling book,' or, 'I was the one who planned that hit new product.' But those are, after all, past accomplishments.

Such people should move on to the next piece of work. Instead, they choose to avoid facing the reality that even if they put in the same effort as before, they might not surpass those past accomplishments. They use the fear of declining ability as an excuse to retreat.

# You Simply Don't Need Inferiority Feelings

Adler believed that everyone has inferiority feelings to some degree. But to face life's tasks, you mustn't allow these feelings to lead to inaction. In fact, you don't need them at all.

Adler distinguished between two kinds of inferiority feelings: the helpful, motivating kind, and the unhelpful, discouraging kind.

Unhelpful inferiority feelings are those that arise when you compare yourself with others. They don't spur you to improve, but trap you in self-consciousness and avoidance. Instead of directing your energy towards action, they direct it towards protecting your pride, which is why they end up being not just unhelpful, but actively obstructive.

Alongside inferiority feelings, Adler also used the term *striving for superiority*, meaning the effort to become better. He then went further, referring to trying to be better than others, which he called *striving for personal superiority*. While some people believe work isn't something you do solely for yourself, it is true that there are those whose only interest in work relates to their own desire to be seen as superior. These people are concerned with nothing *but* themselves, their appetite for beating others and being liked or admired.

Those who chase this personal superiority fear anything that might threaten their advantage. Remember the example at the beginning of this chapter, of the person seeking to feel more capable than a junior colleague by thinking back to their 'better' academic background? A sense of personal superiority is just that; it's a *feeling* of being superior, not actual superiority achieved by getting good results. And superiority gained only through competition and comparison is nothing more than the flip side of an inferiority feeling.

Today, competition in study and work is taken for granted. But if you lose, you're left with inferiority feelings; and even if you win, knowing that you can't keep winning forever leads to a tense, anxious way of living. In Chapter 5, we'll look into what specifically is problematic about competition and whether there are alternatives to competitive relationships.

• • •

Now, the other kind of inferiority feelings Adler described are helpful ones. If inferiority feelings aren't used as a reason to avoid effort, but instead help motivate someone towards meaningful improvement, then they become something useful.

Adler put it this way:

*Neither the striving for superiority nor inferiority feelings are diseases; they are healthy, normal incentives to effort and growth.*

(*What Life Should Mean to You*)

People harbouring inferiority feelings may sometimes see them as pathological, but few would call striving for superiority a disease. More likely, it's the people around someone who is trying too hard to be superior who feel that way.

Here, Adler draws a clear line between healthy forms of inferiority feelings and striving for superiority – those motivations that stimulate effort and growth – and unhealthy ones. Even if you feel inferior, if that feeling drives you to compensate through effort rather than immobilising you in competitive thinking, it should be seen as healthy.

## You Can Make a Healthy Effort
## Without Feeling Inferior First

When I was fifty, I had to be hospitalised after suffering a heart attack. The standard approach to recovery is early mobilisation – while treating the illness, you start rehabilitation as soon as possible. I followed a cardiac rehab programme, gradually increasing how far I could walk. At first, I didn't even leave my hospital room. I started by simply getting out of bed and standing up. I couldn't walk the way I wanted to, but day by day, the distance I could manage grew. Wanting to go from not being able to walk to being able to walk again, and working hard at rehab to make that happen, is what Adler would call a healthy striving for superiority.

That said, I didn't feel inferior because I couldn't walk, nor did I do rehab in order to overcome feelings of inferiority. It's true that I couldn't walk long distances, but that was simply because of illness, rather than personal failing: I *just* couldn't walk. I worked to move from a state where illness prevented me from walking to a state where I could walk again. Therefore, unlike Adler's formulation, I wasn't striving for superiority in order to overcome inferiority feelings.

When you get sick, you seek treatment and rehabilitation in order to return to a healthy state. There's no need to feel inferior by comparing yourself to others, and you're not doing rehab in order to be better than someone else. This leads to a different, uncompetitive form of striving.

It's true that some people *do* feel inferior about things they can't control. Some people, for instance, feel inferior about not being young anymore, but not everyone inevitably develops inferiority feelings as they age. And it's also true that there are things you can no longer do as you get older, but if that's the standard, consider that newborn babies can't do anything at all!

In a similar way, there are also people who feel inferior because they don't know something, but there's no need for that, either. Not knowing something, like not being able to walk, simply means you don't know – it doesn't mean you're inferior. There is no need to manufacture a personal failing out of it. You wouldn't think a child is inferior just because they don't know as much as an adult. No adult knows everything, either, and that doesn't make them inferior. Knowledge can always be gained through learning.

What I want to emphasise is this: you can make healthy efforts without inferiority feelings to drive you. Effort doesn't require inferiority feelings, or a desire to be superior to others.

If you don't know something, you learn it. If your grades aren't good, you study so you can do better next time. That's a useful striving for superiority, and there's no need to tie it to inferiority feelings.

Wanting to learn what you don't know is a fundamental human desire. Trying to gain knowledge, or doing rehab so you can walk again, isn't about overcoming inferiority because you're deficient. Such effort isn't driven by the need to conquer inferiority feelings.

Over time, Adler himself spoke less about inferiority feelings, recognising that the argument that we strive for superiority because we have these feelings makes inferiority seem like the only motivation to strive.

## Why We Always End Up Thinking in
## Terms of Superior and Inferior

As we've just covered, striving for superiority doesn't have to be tied to comparisons with others, competition or notions of better and worse. **It's simply a matter of whether or not you make an effort.** What you're doing and what others are doing are separate things – there's no real meaning in comparing them.

So, why do we end up thinking in terms of superiority and inferiority? Admittedly, Adler's own wording invites that interpretation. He said the following:

*The source of all motivation in human beings, and of all contributions to our culture, is the striving for superiority. The whole of human life proceeds along this broad line of activity – from below to above, from minus to plus, from defeat to victory.*

(What Life Should Mean to You)

Adler's phrasing inevitably evokes images of *up* and *down*, of superiority and inferiority. The problem with putting it this way is that if human life moves from *below*, *minus* and *defeat* towards *above*, *plus* and *victory*, then striving for superiority always seems to begin in a negative, inferior state.

As we've explored, however, not knowing something isn't a minus, nor is being ill. These things are never defeats. Additionally, even if you don't compare yourself with others, you might compare yourself with your ideal self (as we covered on p. 74) and generate inferiority feelings that way. That can also make your current self appear to be in a state of *below*, *minus* or *defeat*.

## You Can Change the Way You Think

If you replace this *up* and *down* with *ahead* and *behind*, and think of each person as moving across a flat plane from their own starting point towards their own goal, then there's no need to think in a hierarchy of superiority and inferiority. Some people are walking ahead, others behind. Some are simply walking quickly, others more slowly.

Even then, you might still be tempted to think that being ahead means being superior. Adler viewed life as movement towards a goal, and he believed that living is a process of evolution. But if you say that living is evolution, then ageing starts to look like degeneration. You may walk quickly when you're young, but as you age, you may no longer be able to walk as fast. Even young people can lose their mobility if they get sick.

When I was in the hospital, I often walked along the corridors connecting different wards. Naturally, everyone else quickly passed me by. But just because I was walking slowly at the back didn't mean I was inferior. And those walking quickly at the front weren't superior. I was simply walking slowly, and simply walking behind.

If you see life as being akin to walking across this flat plane, then how fast you walk or where you are doesn't matter. If simply being ahead is seen as good, however, then competition inevitably arises.

The same is true with studying. Some people feel superior just because they're ahead. I remember classmates in secondary school who would say smugly, 'We already covered that at cram school,' (an after-school programme in Japan where students study ahead of the regular curriculum to prepare for exams) and it was exhausting to listen to. They felt superior because they knew something others had yet to learn. But the truth is that learning earlier doesn't make you superior.

People in front are just in front. People behind are just behind. Fixating on whether you're ahead or behind comes from constantly comparing yourself to others – and there's simply no need for that.

If you can let go of being ahead or behind and accept that it's fine to walk anywhere on the plane, as long as you're making an effort – to be wherever and whoever you are – then you'll be able to accept not just different ways of walking, but also diverse ways of living. This is a key step in letting go of the fear of being ordinary.

5

# APPROACHING YOUR LIFE WITH CONFIDENCE

## The Weight Holding You Down Is Self-made

Up to this point, we've looked at the problems that come with believing you're special. Now, let's move on to how you can approach studying and work with confidence.

To have real confidence, you need to stop standing in your own way. In the previous chapter, we explored how anxiety may be holding you back, because you worry that you won't be able to keep achieving the same kind of success you've had before. As we've seen however, that anxiety doesn't come from declining ability, the appearance of rivals or obstacles suddenly blocking your path. People who fear producing disappointing results can turn anything into a reason not to take on a task – or at least, not to give it their all. No matter what, the only option if someone wants to succeed is to put in the full effort. But in a subconscious attempt to hold that effort back, they manufacture anxiety (see p. 72).

If after trying, you still don't get the results you wanted, you should simply tell yourself, 'I'll do things differently next time and get better results.' That's all there is to it – there is nothing to fear.

And yet, people still stop themselves from taking the first step.

# Competition Isn't a Given

People who consistently deliver good results often *look* confident, but if that confidence comes only from beating others and being recognised through competition, it will disappear the moment they lose.

Even those on top are haunted by the constant fear that they might someday lose, and the moment someone more capable appears, their apparent confidence collapses. It should go without saying that confidence that can be shaken so easily isn't genuine confidence.

In a society where competition is treated as the norm, people come to believe they have no value unless they win, and so, winning is always their goal. But trying to win every time comes with enormous pressure, and even those who have emerged victorious from one intense competition aren't guaranteed to keep winning in the future.

Just because competition is everywhere doesn't mean it's normal. In fact, competition has a very damaging impact on our mental health.

If you want to study and work with confidence, you should step out of the competition. But for people who have lived so long under the assumption that competition is natural, it may be difficult to imagine what it's like to immerse themselves in their work without considering anyone else. Let's explore that now.

# Don't Compare Yourself to Others

To stop worrying about others, you first have to stop comparing yourself to them. You put a lid on your potential whenever you measure yourself against the people around you. If you want to grow your abilities, you have to stop treating others as your yardstick.

The truth is, you don't need to compare yourself to others to be sure of your own excellence. Even if other people do the same kind of work as you do, that doesn't mean you need to examine your work against anyone else's. Some people will always rank work by better or worse, but a person who can confidently say, 'This is the work that's mine to do,' doesn't live by comparisons.

You might wonder if that train of thought leads solely to self-satisfaction. Ideally, your work should also benefit others. But when you become fixated on *proving* that you serve others – to the point of excessive devotion or self-sacrifice – it can start to feel performative rather than genuine.

What's desirable is to first do work that you yourself find fulfilling, and only *then* have that work contribute to others.

Plants don't strive for more once they've borne fruit. People may harvest the fruit or admire the flowers, but that isn't something the plant or flower concerns itself with.

• • •

The reason comparing yourself to others is meaningless is simple: your abilities can't be compared to anyone else's. Musicians don't compete with painters, because the comparison itself would make no sense. In these cases, comparison isn't possible – and neither is envy.

So, what if you're doing the *same* kind of work? Is comparison unavoidable then? When you see someone who seems to breeze through a job similar to yours, you may be tempted to compare their approach with your own. But even if they look like they learn effortlessly and accomplish their tasks with ease, you can't see the time and effort they've put in behind the scenes. After all, unless someone is obsessed with winning against all others, they don't go around advertising how much energy they've put into the task.

When you're oblivious to the struggle and see only the finished result, you end up thinking, *I could never do it like that,* and you stop yourself short, deciding similar feats are impossible for you.

Nothing is achieved without effort. A writer may look like they produce manuscripts with ease, but while a few may write quickly, most don't.

The same thing happens when you see someone who's fluent in a foreign language and think, *I've been studying for years and still can't get there.* You can't see how much time that person has spent learning. When someone reads or speaks effortlessly, it's easy to assume they possess a natural talent. But there's no one who can speak, read or write fluently from the start without effort.

## There's No Need to Compete

As we've seen, people who are afraid of losing in competition may turn away from challenges the moment they're presented with them. They start looking for reasons why they wouldn't win even if they tried to compete, and that becomes their excuse for not engaging with the task at all.

When they do compete, they don't manoeuvre against just anyone. They choose their opponents. They only compete with those they're already convinced they can beat – or at least, those they believe they have a chance of beating.

Thinking this way is ultimately a form of inferiority feeling. No one wants to admit that they're inferior, but it's much easier to tell themselves that they're not competing because the other person is overwhelmingly superior than it is to try and have to face the results.

In the end, the decision as to whether to compete or not depends on the other person – if they're confident they can win, they compete, and if they're not, they don't.

But that isn't the only problem.

. . .

You've no doubt heard Aesop's fable about the tortoise and the hare, in which the two animals decide to settle their argument over which of them is faster with a race.

*The hare, being swift by nature, didn't take the race seriously, wandered off the path, and fell asleep. The tortoise, knowing how slow he was, kept plodding along, passed the hare as he lay resting, and reached the goal to claim victory.*

The hare clearly assumed he would win and so didn't run in earnest, falling asleep partway through. He certainly wouldn't have done that had he been racing an animal faster than himself. Because of his arrogance, the hare suffered an unexpected loss; such is the fable's well-known lesson.

The hare believed there was no way he could lose to the tortoise. For him, the sense of superiority that comes with winning, and the praise of others that follows, were what mattered. If he hadn't thought he could win, no doubt he wouldn't have agreed to race at all. And if it had looked like he was about to lose, he likely would have quit halfway through.

For a long time, I assumed the tortoise must have been calm and unbothered, despite being slow, while it was the hare's arrogance that provided the basis for the story's moral. But when I re-read it, I was surprised to realise that the tortoise, too, had agreed to compete with the hare.

*The tortoise and the hare argued about their speed, set a time and place for the race, and went their separate ways.*

In truth, the tortoise didn't need to rise to the hare's provocation in the first place. Being fast or slow is just a difference – it doesn't establish superiority or inferiority. There was no reason for the tortoise to compete with the hare at all.

The issue isn't choosing not to compete when you think you'll lose. The issue is seeing study and work themselves as competitions. The tortoise kept walking to the end without quitting a race he was expected to lose, but his pace and the hare's were never truly comparable to begin with – the two animals weren't meant to be raced against each other.

That's exactly where the other problem in this story lies: the tortoise accepted the competition when he didn't need to.

# Losing a Competition Doesn't Erase Your Value

If you're anxious about the possibility of losing in competition, what should you do to ease that concern? The answer is simple: *step out of the competition mindset altogether.* Choosing not to think in terms of competition means there is no longer any winning or losing.

Still, some people feel they can't be the only ones to step away. Even if they drop out, others will keep competing, will keep trying to win. And so, people worry that not engaging means losing out.

The idea that everyone is competing is a belief that has been drilled into us since childhood. In reality, however, we're not competing with anyone at all. Once, on a train, I encountered a group of primary-school students on their way to take secondary-school entrance exams. They were wearing head-bands emblazoned with the words *Certain Victory*, their faces tense and grim. If parents and teachers keep telling children that losing a competition means becoming a failure, it's no wonder they grow up thinking exams – and life afterwards – are nothing but struggle.

People who have always found their value by winning

competitions probably can't imagine a life without them, and may never have seriously thought about what would happen if they lost, beyond simply how it would feel. Even so, they likely feel anxious at times about the possibility of losing someday. And anyone who's ever experienced not winning, even once, can't forget the moments during which the competition made them wonder whether they had any value at all. The desire to avoid that feeling again only makes them more desperate not to lose.

Even people who appear supremely confident and seem never to consider losing are, as we've seen, probably living in constant fear of when that loss might finally come. To escape that anxiety, they work hard, because they don't want to lose. But even if they *do* lose, it doesn't mean they've lost their value as a person.

Measuring your worth solely by wins and losses is a profound misconception.

## Instead of Fearing Failure, Learn How to Handle It

We have established that study, work and even life itself aren't competitions – but if you've come to see them that way, how do you shift your thinking and step out of the race?

First, you have to stop being afraid of failure. Failure usually just means there was a problem with how you approached the task; you can learn a better method, train properly and avoid the same mistake next time. When it comes to work, effort is necessary to get good results, but failing doesn't mean you've lost a competition against someone else – and it certainly doesn't mean you should label yourself as worthless.

It's normal for beginners to make mistakes. You can't acquire knowledge without getting things wrong along the way. Yet if, from childhood, you're constantly scolded with comments like, 'Why can't you do this? It's so simple,' you begin to feel that you can't do anything at all, and that anxiety becomes a burden when you face a new task. That's one reason why it's natural to think about how to avoid failure – but you also need to think about what to do when failure happens.

Of course, when you do fail, you have to take responsibility. When a failure occurs, it usually affects other people in addition to yourself, which is why this matters.

First, you should try to restore things as much as you can. If you break an object, complete restoration may be impossible, but if you drop a vase and it shatters, for instance, naturally you start by picking up the pieces and cleaning up. If a surgery goes wrong, you do everything in your power to save the patient's life.

Next, if anyone has been hurt by the failure, you have to apologise. Failure isn't intentional, but an apology to those who were inconvenienced or harmed, in one way or another, is essential.

Finally, you have to think about how to prevent the same failure from happening again. Everyone fails, but if you don't seriously consider how not to repeat the same mistake, you'll end up making it again. Many parents and bosses simply scold children or employees when they fail. That does nothing to prevent future failures. Instead, it may encourage people to focus solely on not getting scolded next time, or even trying to hide their mistakes.

When you fail, you need to take action in these ways, but this is no time to wallow in despair. One failure doesn't mean you can quit working forever. When you fail, you take responsibility – it's as simple as that. There's no need to fear losing your reputation. Hiding a failure destroys trust; taking responsibility for it, on the other hand, usually builds it.

Adler put it this way:

*It is far more important to educate people to be courageous, patient, and confident, and to see failure not as something that crushes courage, but as something to be tackled as a new task.*

(*The Education of Children*)

Modern education doesn't teach this, which is part of the reason why it's so hard to break the habit of competition. Instead, education fixates on results: on whether you succeeded or not. But rather than losing confidence and courage when you fail, you need the strength to work your way through difficulties.

You should, of course, try to avoid failure as much as possible. But when it happens, don't sink into despondency. In fact, it's precisely through failure that you gain the strength to overcome hardship. You should face failure head-on and ask, 'What can I learn from this?'

# Don't Be Afraid of Producing Results

Doing your work will always produce some kind of result. If the task is difficult, you may try and still find you don't complete it. Usually, however, people hesitate in moments like this not simply because the task is not easy – as we've seen, it's because they're afraid of discovering that they might lack ability.

There are people who see someone fail and judge them as incompetent. Yet if you are responsible for work that needs to be done, you have to do it – regardless of what others think of the outcome.

You won't always get good results, but that's something to deal with *after* the results are in. Instead of doing nothing because you fear poor results, or only taking on challenges when you're sure you'll succeed, there are times when you simply have to start without worrying about the outcome.

• • •

The easiest way to avoid producing results is to do nothing at all. As we saw in the example of Adler's daughter on p. 67, the student who's afraid of getting a bad grade can avoid evaluation by skipping the exam. Of course, that means they won't earn credits and won't graduate, so it's nothing more than a temporary escape. If you take on the task, though, you can produce results proportional to your effort. Even if you don't get a perfect score in an exam, you can usually get a very respectable result.

The same applies when trying something new. If you do nothing because you're afraid you won't get good results or that you'll expose your failure, you'll go through life without learning the things that truly matter. In reality, you may get better results than you expected, or find that what you've already learned helps you pick up new lessons and skills more easily than you thought.

You won't know what will happen until you actually try.

## Confidence Has Nothing to Do with Competition

Confidence has nothing to do with success or failure, and people who believe the work they're doing has value don't get caught up in the idea of these things in the first place.

Whatever you do, failure is a part of it. People who have had a relatively smooth run of successes can lose confidence and become afraid of failure the moment things don't go as planned, proving that confidence that *depends* on success disappears the instant you fail.

As we saw earlier, some people avoid seriously engaging with a difficult task precisely so they won't produce results. In the same way, there are people who deliberately decide not to have confidence. You might think, *Who would choose not to be confident?* But if you consider what happens once you *are* confident, you can see why someone might subconsciously hold back.

If you have confidence, you'll take on difficult work. You'll take the exam. You'll put in the effort. And once you do, the results are unavoidable. By contrast, if you do nothing because of a lack of confidence, you don't achieve any results. That's exactly why some people decide not to have confidence – so they can tell themselves they're not trying *because* they lack confidence. This is what it really means to decide not to have confidence – it's just another excuse for someone not to find out what they're capable of.

When you tie confidence to success and failure, it shrivels instantly the moment you tell yourself, 'Trying is pointless. I won't succeed anyway.'

# Don't Say But

If you want to take on challenges without fearing the outcome, you need to decide in advance not to say the word *but*. When there's something you need to tackle and you've already decided not to do it, you'll start saying but, and list reasons why you can't. Saying you *can't* isn't accurate – the truth is you *don't want to*. Most things aren't impossible; we just don't want to do them.

People who say but aren't torn between wanting to try and wanting to avoid it. The moment they say but, they've already decided not to act.

When you feel yourself wanting to say but, the first thing you need to realise is that you simply don't want to do it. The next step is to stop saying but.

There are things you genuinely can't do even if you try. But in a great many cases, you've already decided from the outset that you can't. Sometimes, you start reluctantly, only to find that once you begin, your attitude changes. And some-times, you regret not trying something because by saying 'but', you convinced yourself that there's no way you could do it.

## Don't Live in Possibility

In the preface to *Elements of the Philosophy of Right*, Hegel quoted the following line: 'Here is Rhodes – now jump.'

The source is another of Aesop's fables, which tells the story of a boasting traveller. Constantly subjected to criticism at home for not being manly enough, the man returned home after a long journey overseas. He boasted loudly about his heroic exploits and the fame he had earned in foreign lands, claiming that on the island of Rhodes, he had made a jump so great that no other man could match it. If you went to Rhodes, he said, people at the stadium would testify to it.

At that point, someone interrupted him and said: 'If that's true, you don't need witnesses. Here is Rhodes – now jump.'

I see this man as someone who lives in possibility – someone who only lives fully when action isn't required.

People like this don't want to turn possibility into reality. Many children are told, 'You're smart – you could do it if you tried,' yet they never study. Why? Because as long as they live in the realm of potential, they get to be *a kid who can do it*. They don't want to study, take the test, get a bad grade and be labelled *a kid who can't*.

But results will come eventually, no matter what. Putting off a challenge doesn't change that fact. If you don't get the result you hoped for, all you have to do is try again.

# Focus Only on the Task at Hand

There's a well-known anecdote about the physicist Hideki Yukawa, from the book *What Does It Mean to Grow Up?* One day, while lecturing, Yukawa kept staring at a formula he had written on the blackboard. Then, he said, 'Hold on a moment,' and left the classroom.

He soon returned with a maths professor and asked, right there in front of the students: 'Professor, this looks strange to me — is it wrong?' The professor replied, 'Yes, it's wrong,' and corrected the formula. Yukawa then calmly resumed the lecture.

Shunsuke Tsurumi, who recounted this story, said that while honesty is educationally valuable, teachers who are truly honest are extremely rare. A teacher who openly admits mistakes, like Yukawa, is indeed unusual. The same goes for bosses, politicians and even parents — once they've said something, they may hesitate to admit they're wrong, even when they realise it themselves.

For people who can admit mistakes as frankly as Yukawa, the only thing that matters is solving the task — or at least making progress towards solving it. They don't avoid addressing the problem out of fear of interpersonal friction. If you're constantly worried about what others think, you won't develop real ability in anything you learn.

Earlier, I mentioned a student who refused to translate Greek into Japanese. There's no need to worry about what the teacher thinks. From the teacher's perspective, if they don't know where a student went wrong, they can't teach them. That's why students who stay silent out of fear of being seen as incompetent are the most difficult to deal with.

The same applies in the workplace. New employees are expected to make mistakes. Those who aren't afraid of what their boss thinks grow stronger. Even if the boss scolds them – ignoring their own failure to provide proper guidance – a more junior staff member who asks what went wrong and how to fix it will steadily improve. On the other hand, people who never ask questions because they want to *seem* competent may look good for a while, but they never truly improve.

What matters isn't how you're seen, but what you actually are. To actually *be* capable, you have to accept yourself when you don't know or can't do something. You need to let go of the belief that you have to be special and accept yourself as you are.

Even teachers and bosses make mistakes. When they don't know the answer to a question, they can simply say they'll look it up by next time. Some may question a teacher's ability when they hear this, but refusing to teach falsehoods and committing to the truth is a line no teacher should cross, no matter what their students might think.

Some people prioritise solving the task itself. Others place higher importance on the interpersonal dynamics surrounding it. The latter aren't truly interested in solving the problem – they're obsessed with procedure. They get angry when things move forward without their involvement. These people tend to have a strong sense of pride and won't accept having their mistakes pointed out. Even when a rational solution is presented, they won't accept it unless it was their idea. To them, what matters isn't what was said, but who said it.

Interpersonal conflicts often arise with people like this. If your boss is one of them, directly telling them that they're mistaken will be received like a personal attack. To avoid falling into this mindset yourself, focus not on who said something, but on the content of what was said.

Even when dealing with people who won't admit mistakes, can't accept ignorance or are fixated on procedure, there are times when you have to stand your ground. If you assert yourself, friction is unavoidable. The choice is simple: either you don't assert yourself and avoid friction, or you assert yourself and accept it. There is no option where you assert yourself and friction magically disappears.

Staying silent may temporarily maintain calm and avoid immediate conflict, but it will never lead to real problem-solving.

## You Don't Need Other People's Approval

Work is evaluated, and those evaluations aren't always accurate. What matters is doing good work, not working in order to be evaluated or praised. People who work mainly to gain approval tend to stop working, or stop putting in genuine effort, as soon as they expect they won't be recognised.

You don't have to be special or admired to be valued. If you do good work, people will notice. But once you start working *for* recognition, you lose the ability to do truly good work.

Some people can't feel confident that what they've written (a report or a paper, for instance) is good unless someone else tells them so. But the quality of what you've written and other people's evaluations of it don't always line up.

Throughout history, there have been artists whose paintings weren't highly valued during their lifetimes. Still, whether they were recognised or not, they kept painting. Even when their work didn't sell and they lived in poverty, they themselves saw the value in what they were creating. If being recognised had been their priority, they might have created work that was easier for people to accept at the time. Such work may have been praised by their contemporaries, but it likely wouldn't have had lasting, universal value. After all, countless works of art and literature are forgotten with time.

Some might argue that art is a special case and that evaluating it is uniquely difficult, so it's different from everyday work. But at its core, the relationship between value and evaluation is the same for art and for work. Just as outstanding paintings may go unrecognised during an artist's lifetime, work doesn't lack value if it isn't praised.

What comes first isn't other people's evaluations or approval, but how *you* see it – how *you* feel about it. Evaluation follows as a result. If recognition is your goal, you won't be able to do work that truly has value. Working according to your own standards is what ultimately leads to high appraisals.

## The Crushing Weight of Trying to Be Special

People don't suddenly develop a desire for approval in adulthood. As children, those who earned praise for good grades often studied hard to meet expectations. From the child's perspective, studying in order to win their parents' attention was simply another way of seeking approval. When that praise follows them into adulthood, people may start believing they're special.

But is it really natural – or inevitable – to have this need for approval? When a child who studies well gets good grades and sees their parents pleased, they may study even harder. On the other hand, some children stop studying if they don't get attention. Neither of these reflects what learning should truly be. Whether or not to study is something each person decides for themselves. Letting approval determine this choice makes no sense.

The same is true of work.

Earlier, I mentioned children who are habitually tense due to a belief that they won't be recognised unless they push themselves beyond all reason. Such children, like the girl who went to great lengths to please her teacher on p. 33, tend to lack confidence that they can make a good impression. In school, they aren't confident they'll always get good grades, and they fear that if they don't, their parents or teachers won't think well of them. That's why they become desperate, and end up living tense, pressured lives.

Parents may constantly nag children who don't study, and sometimes end up not paying as much attention to children who study well. As a result, capable children who want their parents' attention push themselves even harder to get higher scores.

The pattern continues when these children grow into adults. They believe they won't be recognised by their boss or colleagues unless they produce good results, and the pressure around work intensifies. It's not that they're incapable – it's the burden of trying to meet others' expectations that weighs on them.

If you believe you have to be recognised as special by others, you'll only be able to do work aimed at gaining that approval. Even when results don't turn out as you hoped, if you stop worrying about what others think, you can decide for yourself how to approach the work – and you can try again next time, with renewed effort.

When you focus on completing the work itself, the need to be special or receive approval fades away. If you stop worrying about others' opinions of you and simply engage with your work, approval and recognition will follow as a natural result.

# Evaluation Doesn't Determine Value

Value leads to recognition – but recognition doesn't define value, especially because others may simply fail to assess the value of your work correctly. When you primarily think about how others will evaluate you, the order is backwards. If you produce good results, recognition follows. Trying to be recognised without any track record simply doesn't make sense. There's no need to go out of your way to impress others with how capable you are.

Adler put it this way:

*Whenever a person feels they need to prove something, they tend to go too far.*

(*The Education of Children*)

As we've already seen with art, the true value of a work isn't always properly acknowledged. It's commonly accepted that truly original, forward-thinking work may not be properly appreciated in its own time. A rating may *seem* correct when many people share the same opinion, but the fact that most people don't rate a work highly doesn't mean it has no value.

Work may not be judged to such wild extremes as art, but the principle is the same. Praise is one indicator of value, but it isn't the whole story. For example, if an evaluation focuses only on the quantity of work produced, and pays no attention to the quality, it may miss the mark entirely.

Of course, being recognised by no one doesn't automatically prove that your work has value. But people who spend all their time thinking about how to be accepted end up doing nothing but people-pleasing work. If they keep that up, they'll eventually lose everyone's trust, just like a yes-person who never disagrees with anyone.

If you approach work the way a test-savvy student tries to guess the examiner's intent in order to give the *right* answer, you may get good test results, but you'll never do truly original work.

Even when your work isn't evaluated fairly, you need to understand that assessment and value don't always align. What matters is having the courage not to be tossed around by other people's opinions.

## When You *Should* Care About How Others See You

All that being said, if lots of people give your work a low evaluation, you should consider the possibility that their feedback contains something useful. When the assessment you're offered is considered and accurate, there are times when you need to humbly accept the criticism and try again.

It's also important to be mindful about how your own words and actions in response to criticism are received by others. After all, you don't want to become a stubborn loner who refuses to listen.

Kiyoshi Miki put it this way:

*Reflection is possible only with a humble heart.*

(Unspoken Philosophy)

When someone points out an issue with your behaviour, you shouldn't brush off their feedback. Instead, humbly reflect on why the observation was made and ask yourself if there really is room for improvement.

A dogmatic person may dismiss such feedback outright, insisting that the criticism is unfounded. When backed into a corner and forced to admit they made an error, some will say, almost as an afterthought, 'It's regrettable that some people chose to make it a problem.' In the end, they're only concerned with how they're perceived, not with examining or correcting their own behaviour.

As long as you believe you're unquestionably right, humility is impossible. You have to allow for the possibility that others may be seeing things correctly. That's what it means to accept the version of yourself that you didn't notice – or didn't want to acknowledge – until someone else pointed it out.

You shouldn't obsess over how others see you. But you also shouldn't cling to self-righteousness. The key is to find the right balance: to act on your convictions while maintaining humility.

# Free Yourself from Other People's Expectations

Some people are high achievers from childhood onward, but that doesn't mean they're always confident or never consider themselves to be failures. As we've seen throughout this book, people like this often live in constant fear that a reversal could happen at any moment.

Adler observed the following:

*During adolescence, one often sees a clear reversal of established tendencies. Children from whom much was expected begin to fall behind in school or work, while those previously thought to lack talent catch up and begin to show unexpected abilities. This does not contradict earlier events. However, there is often a concern that a once-promising child may fail to live up to the expectations they have carried.*

(*What Life Should Mean to You*)

High-achieving children are well aware that such reversals can occur. Even if they look confident, the moment they sense they might lose out in competition, anxiety kicks in and shuts down any attempt at effort.

They don't just fear losing itself. They worry about how their parents will judge them if a younger sibling overtakes them, and about losing the respect of others when they can no longer meet the high standards they once did. As Adler says, they end up crushed by the fear of betraying the expectations that have been placed on them.

No child is immune to failure, but believing that you mustn't disappoint your parents' expectations continuously creates enormous pressure, and children often fear being emotionally abandoned if they fail to live up to them.

And of course, even if you did meet your parents' expectations as a child, there's no guarantee you'll do the same for colleagues, friends and partners as an adult. What you need to realise is this: working only to fulfil others' expectations ignores the evaluation of your work that matters most: your own.

The belief that you mustn't disappoint others can become such a burden that it stops you from functioning. Of course, there's no need to *deliberately* disappoint anyone – all you really need to do is sincerely dedicate yourself to the task at hand. You don't have to think about meeting other people's expectations at all.

. . .

Let's look at the following quote relating to one of Adler's observations from earlier.

*As long as one is supported and praised, one can keep moving forward. But the moment one must rely on one's own effort, courage wanes and one retreats.*

(*What Life Should Mean to You*)

'The moment one must rely on one's own effort' means there will come a time when no one is cheering you on or praising you.

Independence means being able to decide for yourself what and how much to study, even when no one is directing you. But if parents keep praising their child in order to make them study, the child grows into an adult who won't do anything *unless* they're praised. Parents praise their children as a matter of course, but that very behaviour gets in the way of the child's independence.

The same thing happens at work. In your job, there are countless things you have to decide and do on your own, irrespective of whether anyone is watching. You're expected to make an effort, even when no one is praising you or recognising your contribution.

## Asking for Other People's Cooperation

Work requires the resolve to make decisions for yourself, and to take responsibility for the consequences of those decisions. In that sense, work is fundamentally something you do alone. When your own decisions lead to good results, you can genuinely feel that you've drawn on your abilities. When the results aren't good, you can't shift the responsibility on to anyone but yourself.

That said, you can't do every job alone. There are times when you have to ask for other people's cooperation, and there are jobs that can only be completed as a team. If, however, you overemphasise the need for cooperation, your sense of personal responsibility can become murky when things go wrong. Even if a decision was made after consulting everyone, you were still part of the final agreement. The fact that it didn't work out doesn't mean you can pass the responsibility on to others.

In Adlerian psychology, there is a practice called *multiple counselling*, where two or more counsellors work with a single client. If each counsellor has a firm grasp of their own thinking, they can put their ideas on the table and examine them in front of the patient. If none of the counsellors has a clear standpoint of their own, however, they can become mutually dependent and fail to offer the patient a clear perspective.

You might conclude that it would be better to do it alone, but when you work entirely by yourself, you can become self-absorbed and fail to notice your own mistakes. A boss pointing out a junior colleague's error, or vice versa, is an example of good cooperation at work.

There are times when a job goes better when other people are involved in some way. Even if the work is essentially something you perform alone, asking others for their opinions from time to time can help you find a breakthrough when you feel stuck. Still, you will have to take final responsibility for the results, even if they come in part from adopting someone else's opinion. At the same time, you also have to avoid the illusion that you accomplished a job entirely on your own when, in reality, you didn't.

In my case, I write the manuscript, but I can't publish a book solely by my own efforts. I work with an editor to create the book, but the editor isn't making the book alone, either. There are times when my editor's suggestions are perfectly reasonable and yet I don't want to accept them. 'If you're so clever, why don't *you* try writing a book?' is a forbidden line no writer should ever utter – but it's a thought that sometimes crosses my mind.

Whether it's an editor and a writer or any other collaboration, true cooperation requires that each person be independent first, and only *then* work together. If you're dependent, you can't enter into a genuine cooperative relationship. To continue the example, I often write up to a stage close to the final draft on my own, but there are times when I think I should have asked my editor for input much earlier. I used to tell myself that the reason I hesitate to ask for an opinion at an early stage is that I fear my thinking will get knocked off course if I seek outside input before my own ideas are fully formed. As I was writing this book, however, I realised that the real reason is that I see their comments as judgements, and I'm afraid they won't be positive ones.

The editor may not intend their feedback that way, but when I think to myself that I would surely receive a more positive response if I showed them something more complete, I start to hesitate about letting them see the manuscript. As a result, I try to keep it to myself and think it through alone, sometimes wandering into a mental maze. At moments like that, I'm competing with the editor in my own head.

When I calm down, I know I should set aside my pride and focus solely on writing a good book. Still, since there are few editors older than me anymore, I sometimes realise that the younger ones are talented enough to unsettle me.

Asking for other people's cooperation isn't about depending on them – it's about recognising that you often can't do the job to its full potential entirely on your own. Seeking cooperation doesn't mean you lack ability. Any job, when done collaboratively, can bring together each person's strengths and accomplish something that no one individual could do alone.

# Doing *Good* Work

People who do nothing but follow orders eventually find they can't be satisfied unless the work makes sense to them. It's not enough to simply do as you're told and produce results. At the same time, it's not true that anything goes as long as you get results. You have to carefully consider what counts as a *good* result in the first place.

Sometimes, results show up clearly in numbers. In publishing, for example, producing a bestseller is considered important, and the editor behind one is seen as capable – but a book that sells well isn't necessarily a good book. While some books do become bestsellers as a result of their quality, being a bestseller doesn't automatically make a book truly *good*.

Of course, I would be over the moon if a book I wrote became a bestseller. But more than that, I hope the book reaches the people it's meant to reach, and that reading it gives them an opportunity to think about themselves. After all, books *do* have the power to change lives. As an author, that's the kind of book I've always wanted to write.

A conscientious writer won't be satisfied shelving what they truly want – or ought to say – and instead writing a book a certain way simply because they want it to sell, even if it *does* find commercial success. A book that sells but leaves nothing behind in the reader has failed in its purpose.

I don't believe books like that become bestsellers very often, but a writer may want to beat other writers, and an editor may want to beat other publishers by producing a book that flies off the shelves. In Adlerian terms, that's nothing more than a pursuit of personal superiority. Writing and publishing a book that benefits a larger community – *that's* what makes the work truly valuable. Only then can you feel that what you're doing actually matters.

The same can be said for any kind of work. A job may bring profits to your company, but if those profits are harmful to society as a whole, you can't call that good work.

Good work isn't just about doing what you're told, nor is it about doing something only for yourself. Work has value when you can honestly feel that, in some way, it's helping others. Achieving the kind of success that shows up in numbers alone doesn't make it good work.

# Doing Work That Only You Can Do

We've talked a fair amount about not needing to be special and focusing on the uniqueness of the work you can do. Still, if you overemphasise the idea that you're irreplaceable, you may end up treating yourself as special.

No two people can do the job in exactly the same way, but if there's no one who can step in, that means you can't take a break or go off sick – and if one person leaves, the organisation ceases to function as it should, without someone else to take over. To train the next generation, you have to assume that a job isn't something only one specific person can do.

And yet, there *is* work that only you can do. Even when a job itself is the same, how to approach it differs from person to person. The procedures may be spelled out in a manual, but flexible responses and personal ingenuity are still required.

It's precisely because you can exercise your own judgement that work feels worthwhile. If you believe that anyone could do your job just as well as you do, it's hard to feel motivated. Of course, you can't decide everything entirely on your own, but if you have to follow your boss's instructions on every single detail, your work can't possibly be interesting.

Teaching others your own, personal way of doing things doesn't mean the originality of your work – or your approach to it – will be lost. Simply copying the steps to be taken doesn't enable someone else to do the job in the same way.

You can't create work out of nothing, so some degree of codifying your approach is necessary. But merely imitating others will never lead to creative work.

What's important to keep in mind here is that originality doesn't mean doing something no one has ever done before. Creativity begins by adding small changes to the experience and knowledge that so many people before you have built up.

Throughout his life, the philosopher Takeshi Umehara was known for having conducted original research across a great many fields, but few people may know that he studied Greek philosophy when he was a student. After reading Umehara's graduation thesis, his advisor, Michitaro Tanaka, remarked, 'This thesis is *hineinlegen,* but the interpretation of classics must be *auslegen.*' In literary theory, *hineinlegen* means putting one's own feelings and ideas into the text, while *auslegen* means drawing out its meaning.

Tanaka told Umehara that he mustn't insert his own ideas into the literature (*hineinlegen*), but instead conduct research in which understanding naturally emerges from the text itself (*auslegen*). Umehara acknowledged that this critique was fair, but wrote, 'I was more eager to gain confirmation of my own way of living than to objectively understand another person's philosophy' (*The Structure of Laughter*). He eventually left Tanaka's supervision.

When I joined the same department later on, I, too, read a great many Greek philosophical texts in the original language. We were required to read them with absolute precision, not overlooking a single word, and we were forbidden from injecting our own interpretations.

When I was young, I wanted to think more freely, so I sympathised with what Umehara was saying. But I came to learn that you can't think freely out of nothing, and that it's crucial to think within constraints sometimes in order to read philosophical texts accurately.

It's like how a bird can't fly in a vacuum: it needs the resistance provided by the air to stay aloft. Research is the same. Originality doesn't arise from nothing.

. . .

If you focus only on doing things differently from others, you'll never do truly original work – work that only you can do. What matters isn't trying to be different from everyone. That, too, is just another form of pursuing your own feeling of personal superiority.

In any kind of work, doing what only you can do isn't about showing off how superior you are. Rather, it calls for thinking about how you can be of use to others. If instead of just doing what's required, you ask yourself whether there's something more you can contribute to the people involved in your work, even routine tasks can feel different from day to day.

Originality is about creating value. New ideas and ingenuity grow precisely out of a conscious awareness of contributing to others and to society. By adding your own perspective and refinements to existing frameworks and procedures, your work becomes something uniquely yours.

It's because of this sense of contribution that you can have confidence in yourself and feel that the work you're doing has value. It's precisely that feeling that tells you you don't have to be special – that it's okay to be just the way you are.

# Listening to Your Vocation

The poet Rainer Maria Rilke, upon receiving some poems from a young writer named Franz Xaver Kappus, told him to stop seeking criticism altogether. Instead, he advised him to ask himself, in the quietest hour of the night: 'Must I write?' (*Letters to a Young Poet*).

And if, after asking 'Must I write?' he could answer, 'I must,' then, Rilke said, 'Build your life according to this necessity.'

What Rilke means by 'I must write' is expressed in German as *Ich muß schreiben*, which can also be translated as 'I have to write'. But this doesn't mean writing out of a sense of obligation – it means writing in response to an inner prompting.

If you feel that you *must* write, then there's nothing to do but write. Whether the poem will sell or not doesn't matter. If you don't write unless it sells, then you're not writing in response to an inner prompting.

Rilke also advised Kappus to stop comparing his poems to those of others, and to stop worrying about being rejected after sending them to publishers.

If you write poetry in accordance with an inner prompting or a sense of necessity – in other words, because you *must* write – then other people's evaluations cease to matter, and you stop riding the emotional roller coaster of praise and criticism.

That said, we are all concerned with how others will judge us. I'm not a poet, but as mentioned earlier, I sometimes worry that a manuscript I send to an editor might be rejected. Still, Rilke's advice to the young writer was to stop even sending his work out.

Writing poetry might not lead to worldly success. Of course, Rilke himself must have written it because he couldn't help it. Yet his poetry collections didn't sell. In fact, he once wrote back to Kappus that he wanted to give him a copy of his book but couldn't afford to buy it himself, and asked him to pick one up at a bookshop if he happened to find it.

The moment you find yourself thinking, *Will this poem sell?* your way of life has already drifted away from the necessity of *having to* write.

In English, a vocation is called a calling; in German, it's *Beruf.* Both words mean 'being called by God'. Of course, unless you're a person of faith, you probably don't think of your current job as something you were literally summoned to do by God. Yet many people will have experienced working with a sense of mission.

The English word 'responsibility' comes from 'response' and 'ability' – the ability to respond. When someone who sees their work as a vocation is asked, 'Who will take on this task?' they answer voluntarily, 'I will.' Responding to a call – this is what true responsibility means. And the work you accept in that way becomes your vocation.

Only work you take on willingly, guided not by mere obligation but by an inner prompting, deserves to be called a vocation.

When you think, *This is something I can't not do*, that feeling comes not from duty, but from a sense of mission or a powerful inner motivation.

Still, even people who actively take on work don't always see it as their vocation. The philosopher Jean Guitton drew a distinction between vocation and ambition, and said we should ask ourselves which we are following:

> *Ambition is anxiety. Vocation is expectation. Ambition is fear. Vocation is joy. Ambition calculates and fails. And success is the most dazzling of all its failures. Vocation abandons itself to nature, and everything is given to it.*
>
> (*My Philosophical Testament*)

Ambition is anxious and fearful because it seeks recognition from others. Such people, as Alfred Adler put it, boast 'proudly of how ambitious they are', using ambition as a 'beautiful-sounding word' (*Understanding Human Nature*). But when they fear that their abilities may fall short and that hard work won't produce good results, anxiety sets in. In this case, ambition is nothing more than vanity dressed up to look impressive.

Adler said that vanity 'has never given direction to human beings, nor has it given them the power to lead to useful achievements' (*Understanding Human Nature*). Useful achievements must benefit not only one's own company, but a larger community as well. Even if you succeed at work purely to gain recognition, that success is not a useful achievement, but merely a crystallisation of vanity.

What you are working on now, or what you are about to take on – can it truly be called a vocation?

# 6

# STARTING FROM WHO YOU ARE

## Accepting the Real You

When it comes to studying or working, nothing gets accomplished if you do nothing. Effort is unavoidable, and yet when you say, 'You don't have to be special – it's enough to be ordinary,' some people push back. That resistance comes from the fear that if they accept themselves as they are, they'll stop trying.

In study and work alike, it's impossible to know everything from the outset. Most of us keep working to acquire knowledge not only during our student days, but even after we start our careers. Some of the knowledge we picked up whe we were young may not always stay relevant.

If the real you is someone who doesn't know certain things, then accepting yourself as you are means accepting that reality of not knowing, and starting from there. You have to begin by acknowledging that there are still things you don't know. Not knowing, by itself, doesn't force anyone to stop – it's the fear of what not knowing might mean that leads people to hold back.

And yet, among those who see themselves as special, there are people who refuse to admit that there are things they don't know. It takes courage to admit ignorance, but it's precisely because there are things you don't know that you feel motivated to learn. Once you start believing that you already understand everything, you stop trying to learn, and your growth stalls.

On the other hand, people who lack confidence in their own abilities and push themselves to extremes also fail to accept themselves as they are. We've already seen how such people fear being judged and try to present themselves in a positive light. They, too, need to assess their current abilities realistically and put in the necessary effort without stressing about how others see them.

You may worry about what people will think when they see what you don't know, but more than that, it's common not to want to accept *yourself* as not having the answers, or as someone who isn't good at studying or work. When I was young and preparing for entrance exams, I took mock exams repeatedly. I took these tests to gauge whether I could get into the university I hoped for based on the results – but that wasn't all. By taking those mock exams, I could find out precisely what I still didn't fully understand.

None the less, I was afraid of grading my exams and discovering that my scores were poor, so I avoided scoring them myself. I was scared of being forced to face the reality of what I didn't yet know head-on. But avoiding that truth meant there was no way my abilities could improve.

By contrast, many of my classmates graded their exams immediately afterwards. Even if their scores were low, they calmly identified their weak points and worked to improve.

In cases such as these, what matters most is producing results on the real exam – and knowing your weaknesses through mock exams is absolutely essential to getting into college. Yet, lacking the courage to accept who I really was, I clung to a groundless sense of pride that I was somehow special. If I didn't know my results, I could still imagine I had done perfectly.

By refusing to accept who I was, I obstructed my own chances of improvement.

# Knowing That You Don't Know

Only those who accept that there are things they don't know will actively try to learn. You'll have no doubt heard of the word *philosophy*, which in ancient Greek means the love of wisdom, from *philo-* (loving) and *sophia* (wisdom).

The lover of wisdom is not a self-proclaimed expert. People who think they know nothing don't try to learn, and people who think they know everything don't feel the need to. The lover of wisdom keeps learning precisely because they assume neither. They avoid both extremes: despairing over ignorance and assuming complete knowledge. By acknowledging what they don't yet know, they're motivated to keep learning, and that willingness to learn is the essence of philosophy as the love of wisdom.

People who acknowledge there are things they don't know are able to approach life with humility. Those who aren't humble, by contrast, see knowledge as proof of their own superiority. For them, knowledge is a means to stay one step ahead of others, and they may flaunt their supposed excellence over those who don't know as much as they do.

As a result, when they encounter someone who knows more than they do, they feel inferior. And when there's something they don't know, they try to hide it, or pretend they know even when they don't.

## You Can Only Start from What You Can Do

There are three types of things in the world: those you *should* do, those you *want* to do and those you *can* do. Of these, the only kind you can actually work on are the things you *can* do.

The truth is, lofty goals often don't translate into action. When you learn something new, you need to accurately assess your current ability. If you tell yourself, 'I don't want to start with something easy,' you won't make any real progress. Even if you want to do more, you can only work with what you're able to do right now.

When you come across a task that seems impossible at your current level, you can't afford to give up simply because you lack the knowledge needed to complete it. It may feel out of reach, but your only option is to start, however slightly, from what you *can* do.

By studying, you can move beyond your initial state of ignorance. Do nothing, and you gain nothing. The same rule applies at work. When you first join a company, there's almost nothing you know, but all learning happens little by little. Instead of deciding from the start that you can't do it, or that you can't compete with others, if you begin with even the smallest thing you *can* do, you'll often find that you end up accomplishing far more than you expected.

People who give up right away aren't avoiding action because the work is truly too difficult. They're putting the brakes on their own effort by convincing themselves they *can't* do it.

Some people won't even attempt a task unless they believe they can score a perfect hundred per cent, even though, with effort, they could perhaps get at least sixty. Borrowing Adler's phrase, they fall into 'all-or-nothing' thinking (*The Education of Children*). In other words: if they can't get the result they want, they do nothing at all. But studying *does* move you out of ignorance. That's a simple fact.

## Moving Beyond Fear Towards Growth

Ignorance isn't inferiority, but merely a starting point. You're bound to make mistakes whenever you start learning something new, precisely because there's so much you don't yet know.

As I've mentioned, I used to teach Greek at a Japanese university. Greek is often treated as the very symbol of an incomprehensible language, as in the English idiom: 'It's all Greek to me.' Given that reputation, it's only natural for beginners to make mistakes.

I wrote earlier about a student who refused to answer when called upon. In class, I would have students translate Greek practice sentences into Japanese and then explain any mistakes. But when this student's turn came, they fell silent. Later, when I asked why they hadn't answered, they said, 'I didn't want you to think I couldn't do it.'

I had to promise them, 'I won't think you're incapable just because you got a problem wrong.' After that, they started answering without fear of making mistakes, and their skills steadily improved. Anyone who has studied a foreign language probably knows that it's precisely when you make mistakes that new information really sticks.

This student may have been encountering, for the first time, the experience of facing a problem they couldn't read or understand. Their concern about how the teacher would see them is clear from their comment about not wanting to be seen as incapable. Even though mistakes were inevitable, seeing other students in the same class answer with apparent ease (even if it certainly wasn't as easy as it may have seemed) made them feel inferior.

While teachers don't play favourites with their students, the situation may have felt like that of a firstborn child when a younger sibling enters the scene – as if the teacher's attention was focused only on those more capable, and the student who had once been the best had been knocked off their throne.

You may want to outperform other students and earn the teacher's approval, but when you can't beat others and feel like you're failing to meet expectations, you can find yourself giving up on studying altogether. Ultimately, however, the only thing that truly matters is building your ability. Learning alongside others inevitably invites comparison, but some people learn faster and others more slowly – that's all. Neither is inherently superior.

Like the student mentioned above, people freeze in front of a task because they're afraid of being seen as ignorant. But learning itself is the process of facing that real, unknowing self and growing past it. Stepping forward without fear of failure is the only way to expand your horizons.

## Have the Courage to Accept That
## You Can Always Know More

Once, I realised that a medication a doctor had prescribed for me didn't interact well with a heart medicine I had been taking for several years, so I asked them to change it. When I explained the reason for this to the pharmacist who checked the prescription, they replied that they had never heard of such a thing, and that there was no problem. I remember being taken aback.

These days, it's easy to gather information on the internet. You can research medications both before and after seeing a doctor. But online information isn't always accurate, so our best choice is still to rely on professionals – in this case, doctors and pharmacists. That being said, if something goes wrong, it's the patient who suffers, which is why you can't just leave everything entirely to others.

The medication the doctor initially gave me was a standard one – something any doctor would prescribe if they didn't know about my condition in detail. Prescribing it didn't mean the doctor was wrong. However, if a pharmacist doesn't find a patient's explanation convincing and wants to change their mind, they shouldn't simply assert their own expertise. They need to offer a logical explanation, one that the patient can actually accept.

If this had truly been the first time the pharmacist had heard of such an issue, they could have checked the drug's contra-indications on the spot. But this pharmacist, who declared there was no problem without even stopping to check, seemed not to doubt their own knowledge.

Confidence born of competence can make others uneasy. Even experts need to avoid assuming that their knowledge is absolute. Those who think they already know everything stop seeking further knowledge and stop listening to those around them. It's only because we recognise that there is always more to discover that we can be always learning.

Those who are genuinely confident are humble. Knowledge acquired when you're young can eventually become obsolete. In fields that advance at breakneck speed, like medicine, you may even discover that what you once knew is now considered wrong. But admitting a mistake never means admitting incompetence. On the contrary, it's essential for acquiring correct knowledge. Only by acknowledging our errors can we deepen our understanding and continue to grow.

Not knowing is never a sign of inferiority. By the same token, having knowledge doesn't automatically make you superior. It simply means you had an opportunity to learn something the other person didn't. Teachers know more than their students for one simple reason – they have had more time to learn.

## Stop Trying to Make Yourself
## Look Better Than You Are

Trying to make yourself look better than you are is nothing more than vanity. If you want to study or work without being paralysed by fear of the outcome, you have to drop that conceit and start by accepting yourself as you are.

In any endeavour, if your abilities aren't fully developed yet, you have to acknowledge your current level and start from there. But if you succeed in making others believe you're more capable than you really are, you'll then have to live up to that image – and that's when the pressure really kicks in.

I'm reminded of the summer of my third year in high school, when I attended supplementary classes in English composition. Students were handed worksheets, and asked to translate the problems into English, then called on to write their answers on the board. The teacher would then provide full explanations and revise the compositions.

Looking at one of those worksheets, I suspected the teacher hadn't written the problem himself. To check, I went to a bookshop after class. I picked up several English composition workbooks and quickly found one that contained the exact same problem as the one in our handout.

I bought the book, and while preparing for next day's class, I found myself wanting to look at the answer key that came with it. I told myself I shouldn't look at it right away, but I rationalised what I was doing by telling myself I would only look after writing my own compositions. Yet once I'd looked at the first answer, there was no turning back. I revised my writing using the model answers as a reference, telling myself that I wasn't copying, that I was only using them as a guide, and I took my work to class the next day.

The teacher didn't correct any of my work, owing to the fact that I had written with the help of the answers. Instead, he said to me, 'This is good.' I was already fairly good at English to begin with, but once he said that, I felt obligated to live up to his expectations. Being thought of as a capable student didn't actually improve my English skills, but at that time, what mattered most to me was being *seen* as someone who could complete the tasks well.

I never bragged about receiving that praise. Still, I couldn't accept the version of myself who would make mistakes if I wrote in English on my own. I became afraid of making errors, and I think that's why my English ability stopped improving. Instead of trying to make myself look capable when I wasn't, I should have accepted the self who didn't know, the self who couldn't do it yet. Only then could I have learned without fearing every misstep.

People who try to make themselves look good, or who believe others see them as competent and knowledgeable, end up desperately trying to live up to that image. They become trapped by others' perceptions of them as capable, which prevents them from bringing out their true abilities.

But once you realise that making mistakes won't automatically label you as incompetent, you no longer feel the need to force out the right answer at all costs. You can take your time, learn properly and steadily build your abilities.

## Stop Being Preoccupied with Yourself

As I mentioned earlier when discussing people who get habitually tense, those who fear failure and mistakes are ultimately afraid of other people seeing them as incompetent. In that sense, they're preoccupied with how they're perceived, trying to live up to others' expectations of them being capable.

Such people aren't truly interested in the work itself, so if they put in effort and aren't recognised for it, they lose motivation. Afraid of not being acknowledged despite their efforts, they prefer to live in the hypothetical world of 'If only I'd tried harder, I would have been recognised.' Unconsciously, they stop themselves from actively engaging with the work. Needless to say, that line of reasoning doesn't hold water with anyone else.

Work is work, and results will always be evaluated. Nonetheless, it's a mistake to focus on how *you* are evaluated rather than on the results themselves.

Making a mistake doesn't turn you into a failure. Feeling as though others might see you that way is often just an excuse to shy away from the task at hand because you don't want to be viewed negatively.

The Greek classes I taught had only a handful of students each year – five in a good year, sometimes just one. You might assume that students afraid of making mistakes would speak up even less in a large class, or that standing out in a small one would feel especially uncomfortable. But whatever the size, there's no need to worry about the opinions of others when you make an error.

The same dynamic appears in corporate training sessions. Many people stay silent, worried about what colleagues or supervisors will think if they ask a question. When questions are anonymous, participation rises. When faces are visible, participants imagine others thinking, *You didn't know that?* Some simply don't want their beliefs or thinking exposed through their questions.

I've given lectures at training seminars for national civil servants several times. On occasion, supervisors would line up along the back of the room. It always comes as a relief when someone summons the courage to ask a question in that kind of atmosphere, and I would always feel a weight lift when a participant spoke up, but people who can do that are rare. It's an organisational problem when employees feel they have to read the room and watch their superiors' expressions instead of saying what needs to be said.

People who are overly concerned with how others see them – people who are fixated on themselves – need to shift their focus away from thoughts of their status and towards the tasks at hand, the results of their work and the meaning of what they're doing.

# Don't Let Anyone Else Decide
# What You Can and Can't Do

Some teachers may label a student who makes a mistake as simply incapable of learning. But making a mistake does not mean a student is incapable.

Likewise, a boss might be overly critical with a colleague who has underperformed in some way, berating them as useless or incompetent, but all that really means is that they failed *this* time. It's wrong to conclude that they're an incapable employee.

When a teacher or a boss chews you out, you have to tell yourself, 'I only made this mistake because I didn't know enough,' or 'I only failed *this* time' – not that you're incompetent.

Of course, results matter in work and at school, so evaluation is unavoidable. If you receive a low assessment, all you can do is try harder next time. There are times, however, when you may be given an unfair evaluation or written off with a careless remark, and you need to take care not to let such incidents rob you of your motivation to work.

Adler calls this the *second battlefield*: situations outside the work itself where people in authority try to raise their own value by lowering that of others. The *first battlefield*, in his terms, is the work itself. Personally, I think calling work a battle-field is a mistake, but setting that aside, the second battlefield refers to moments when a superior harshly scolds a capable staff member for a small mistake in order to elevate themselves by comparison. People who behave this way lack confidence. They're simply trying to boost their own self-perceived value by tearing down others. You mustn't let teachers or bosses like that crush your courage.

That said, thankfully not all educators or managers are like this. Some don't jump to unfair conclusions when students or staff perform poorly. Instead, they realise there may be problems with their own instruction, and they work to improve it.

Adler put it this way:

*I do not believe in a child's ability or lack thereof. What exists is only the teacher's ability or lack thereof.*

(Children with Behavioural Problems)

If the person in that role ignores their own shortcomings and scolds you as incompetent when you slip up or don't improve, you don't have to take it to heart. What matters is continuing to make positive efforts so that you yourself can progress.

# Enjoy the Process of Learning

I casually used the word *progress* just now, but if you start thinking that being able to move ahead faster makes you more capable, learning turns into a competition, and your attention narrows to the outcome.

Many people see university-entrance or job exams as competitions – you have to answer accurately in a short amount of time and get a good score to pass. To do that efficiently, you need to learn techniques for quickly skimming and interpreting questions rather than thinking them through carefully. Students preparing for university-entrance exams are taught these techniques by their teachers. If you feel like this kind of studying isn't particularly fun – well, I would have to say that reaction is perfectly valid.

Exams like entrance tests always have correct answers. But in the real world, there are often questions with *no* clear answers, and situations where you're expected to arrive at your own answer without relying on others' opinions or past solutions. In those cases, if you can't enjoy the process of getting *to* an answer (rather than merely getting the answer itself), both studying and work become painful chores.

For people who have been competing since their student days, enjoying the learning process may be difficult. They may have studied by sheer force just to get results. Especially in situations where those results had to be produced in a limited time span, they may not have even considered the idea that learning could be enjoyable.

Still, as demanding as studying for exams or certifications may be, it's hard to keep going unless you can feel the joy of learning something new along the way. If you focus only on results and feel no satisfaction in the learning or training process itself, you'll lose motivation the moment you fail to get the result you wanted.

To enjoy the learning process, you need to actually experience the joy of discovering what you didn't know. Take foreign-language learning, for example: at first, it takes a long time to read and understand sentences; gradually, however, you realise you can read faster. It's precisely that kind of enjoyment in learning that ultimately leads to accomplishing your goals.

# Learn Slowly

People who have been competing since childhood often believe that nothing can be achieved without rivalry. But even exams, which might seem at first like the ultimate contests, aren't truly battles against other people.

It's true that in selective exams like entrance tests, you're not guaranteed to pass, no matter how hard you try. But acquiring knowledge for those exams has nothing to do with competing against other people. Even when you're studying for a test, learning something you didn't know should be inherently enjoyable. Yet once you think you have to beat others, the joy of learning disappears.

Those who assume competition is the norm end up seeing both study and work as contests. But neither inherently requires you to compete. Effort isn't something you make just to win a competition. You may not know whether it will pay off, but one thing is certain – without it, you won't accomplish anything at all. This is precisely why we *do* make the effort.

Learning something you didn't know should be a source of joy in and of itself. Competition, however, robs you of that joy. If studying for exams was a painful experience for you, it's because your mind was fixated on the competitive aspect of the test, and you shut your eyes to the joy of learning.

People who make an effort know, in Adler's words, that 'what matters is not what one is given, but how one uses what one has been given' (*Problems of Neurosis*). When learning, some people move forward quickly, while others take more time. To say that some people need more time can make it sound as if learning quickly is superior, but the difference between learning quickly and learning slowly isn't about superiority or inferiority – it's simply a difference in *how* you learn. If it takes time for you to learn, then take the time.

To those who value efficiency, taking time over a task may look like a waste. But there are a great many things you can't truly acquire unless you invest the time. People who prioritise efficiency tend to give up if they don't understand something right away. They've probably never had the experience of understanding something *because* they took their time, nor the realisation of how much fun spending that time can be.

Efficiency-minded people think they have to acquire knowledge faster than others. To free yourself from the mindset of competition, you need to intentionally give yourself the experience of slow learning.

People who are good at their jobs *do* put in effort. That effort, however, often isn't visible from the outside. As mentioned earlier, truly capable people don't brag about how hard they've been working. And it certainly isn't the case that everyone who is good at their job acquired the necessary knowledge efficiently and effortlessly.

Finishing work quickly doesn't necessarily mean someone is competent. If you focus only on speed, you may find yourself making more mistakes, and new knowledge may fail to truly sink in.

Trying to be as efficient as possible and focusing on nothing but producing an answer is mechanical. Machines operate *only* for a specific purpose. People are different.

People are also goal-oriented in the sense that they set objectives and move towards completing them. But on the way to achieving those goals, they don't do *only* what's directly useful for that single purpose.

The ability to do things that may seem pointless at first glance is what distinguishes people from machines. Learning is no different. If you're not fixated solely on achieving a goal and instead take the time to enjoy the learning process itself, it can lead to unexpected, creative insights.

# Start Something New

I believe there's great value in learning something new after you've entered the workforce. And even more so as you get older. It doesn't have to be directly useful for your job, and it doesn't have to be immediately practical. Simply trying something you've never challenged yourself with before can change how you feel day to day.

In my case, I started learning Korean after I turned sixty. My speciality was Western philosophy, so I studied a fair few European languages when I was young, but Korean was my first encounter with an Asian language. After finishing basic grammar with a Korean teacher, I moved on to reading essays by the author Kim Yeonsu.

As you would expect, I made mistake after mistake at first. I prepared carefully between classes, but when I translated the Korean passages into Japanese in front of my teacher, I made errors I had never made in any other language.

I had taught Greek at a university for many years, but once I became the learner, I finally understood how my students must have felt. I found I was repeating to myself what I had once told them: 'Just because you get this or that problem wrong doesn't mean you're a bad student.' I had to remind myself that mistakes didn't mean I couldn't do it or that I lacked ability – it just meant I had made a mistake.

At first, I couldn't quite bring myself to admit that I would inevitably stumble. But over time, I came to think mistakes are natural for beginners, and I stopped worrying so much when I got things wrong.

Learning something new is supposed to be enjoyable. If it doesn't feel that way, it's because you're fixated on competing. In my case, the lessons were one-on-one, so there were no other students. And yet, I still imagined a fictional student who was better than me, and I found myself competing against this flawless, imaginary person.

Becoming a learner also made me realise something else. Yes, when I didn't understand something right away, it was partly because I hadn't studied thoroughly enough. However, I also found myself paying more attention to *how* things were taught. After all, when you study with multiple instructors, you can really spot the difference between good and poor teaching.

This insight is also useful when you're in a position where you're responsible for someone else. When a boss has personal experience as a learner, for example, they're less likely to blame an employee's failure on lack of ability or effort alone. Instead, they'll reflect on whether there might be room to improve their own teaching approach. As a result, rather than snapping, 'Why can't you do this?' they're more likely to choose their words carefully and give appropriate guidance.

You also realise that you've quietly forgotten how hard it was when you yourself were struggling to learn something new. Whenever you feel like saying to someone, 'Why can't you do this?' you need to remember, through the experience of trying something new, that you once went through the exact same thing.

Effort is essential, whatever the subject. But the experience of gradually acquiring new knowledge, and the joy you feel while learning, naturally spreads to those around you. If learning feels like nothing but pain, the problem lies in *how* you're learning, or in the preconceived notions you're bringing to it.

If you haven't personally experienced the joy of discovering something you didn't know, you can't convey that to others. As tough as things may feel at the beginning, so long as you don't give up and keep at it, results will appear sooner than you expect. It's precisely through these personal experiences that you can pass on the joy of learning to other people.

This applies far beyond boss–junior dynamics. Whenever you learn something on your own initiative, it's important not to do so with a competitive mindset and to enjoy learning for its own sake. These days, more people study independently, and technologies like language-learning apps often build in systems that pit learners against one another. I can't get on board with that kind of competition.

. . .

Learning isn't about beating other people – it's about personal growth.

# Value the Process, Not Just the Outcome

At work, you're expected to produce results, but results aren't the only thing that matters. As we've seen, there are healthy ways to pursue excellence, and there are misguided ones.

Pursuing a sense of superiority solely for your own benefit is the wrong path. This kind of pursuit shows up as what we call *ambition*. Adler warned that children with excessive ambition tend to end up in difficult situations.

> This is because it has become habitual to judge by the result – by whether one has succeeded or not – and not by the capacity to face difficulties and overcome them. In our civilisation, it has become customary to be more interested in visible results and success than in fundamental education.

(*The Education of Children*)

Even if you believe that results are all that matter – and even if you *do* achieve good results – Adler pointed out that 'success obtained with little effort is easily lost' (*The Education of Children*).

Of course, some people succeed through sustained effort. But once you have an experience like getting lucky on an exam and scoring well, your attention shifts to how cleverly you can produce results. Before long, you start thinking that results alone are enough. Conversely, if you think you won't get results, you may stop trying before you even begin.

Producing results is important, but you can't *always* get good results. Parents and teachers sometimes say things like, 'You worked hard, but results like this aren't good enough,' crushing a child's courage and ignoring the entirety of the process that led there. As the person directly involved, all you can do is focus on how hard you yourself worked and continue making the effort to see the task through.

• • •

If you still feel unsatisfied after achieving your goals, that's a problem, especially if you start craving praise and approval.

> *Even when a child succeeds, they are not satisfied unless people recognise their success. Often, when difficulties arise, maintaining mental balance becomes more important to the child than actually attempting to overcome the difficulty. A child forced down the path of ambition doesn't realise this, and they consequently struggle to live without constant praise. As a result, many children become dependent on the opinions of others.*
>
> (*The Education of Children*)

You may get the results you want, but they don't feel like enough, and your desire to be praised and recognised by others grows all the stronger. As a result, your behaviour becomes swayed by other people's opinions, and you lose the ability to make your own decisions.

Of course, you may act entirely on your own judgement and still fail. When that happens, some people dodge responsibility, coming out with excuses like, 'I didn't really want to do it anyway.'

. . .

If you don't shift blame and instead accept failure as an essential part of the process, it becomes not an obstacle, but a source of insight. To make that shift, you must have the courage to accept yourself as the ordinary person you are. More than any single success, this is what allows for real growth.

# 7

# LIVING YOUR OWN LIFE

# Being Ordinary in Relationships

Looking back at what we've discussed so far, being ordinary doesn't mean being the same as everyone else. In fact, you *shouldn't* be the same; but that doesn't mean you have to be special, either.

So, what should you do? Live as yourself – as someone who is *different* from anyone else.

Naturally, you may still encounter people who demand that you be special, or who pressure you to succeed, but their expectations don't have to define the way you live.

And of course, some people seek safety in being the same as everyone else. Afraid of failing if they hold their own opinions and make their own decisions, they choose to live in the same way as the people around them, following the path laid out by their parents or other adult role models. Such individuals never push back, and as a result, they fail to realise that their life choices have been severely limited.

In this chapter, we'll consider how to live your own life as you truly are, rather than as the person others expect you to be.

# Stumbling in Relationships

In the previous chapter, we looked at what to do when you encounter things you don't know. But when it comes to how to live your life, there are also a great many things we don't know without learning. One of these is how to relate to other people; to live your own life, you need to know how to build good relationships.

There's no job that's done entirely alone from start to finish, and in this way, work, too, is all about relationships. Even if you usually work by yourself and can complete tasks independently, all jobs require at least some amount of interaction with other people. It's no exaggeration to say that if you can't build relationships, you can't do good work. At the very least, believing that your co-workers don't dislike you is key to collaborating smoothly.

The fact that some people who are supposedly competent engage in bullying or intimidation (as we saw on p. 155) is also a relationship issue. A superior who scolds their junior colleagues may think they can control those around them, but in reality, they just don't know how to build good relationships with their team.

. . .

In essence, being good at your job and being respected by those around you are two different things. No matter how capable you are, if you neglect your relationships, you won't earn genuine respect.

# Self-worth Is the Doorway to Every Relationship

Entering relationships takes courage. No one can live entirely alone, therefore it's impossible to avoid interpersonal relationships. Relationships, however, can be tricky. Friction arises in one way or another whenever you interact with others, and sometimes, people get hurt.

It's not an exaggeration to say that there are no worries unrelated to relationships. Relationships are the source of nearly all our troubles.

As I've quoted several times now:

*You can have courage only when you feel that you have worth.*

(*Adler Speaks: The Lectures of Alfred Adler*)

You can't survive without human connection, and the joy and happiness of living can only be felt within relationships. To experience that joy and happiness, **you need the courage to engage with others.**

The first step in building that courage is to believe that you have value. At work, feeling valuable means believing you're competent. In relationships, feeling valuable means liking who you are. If the word *like* feels uncomfortable, you can think of it as being able to accept yourself. Even if you don't like yourself outright, if you can recognise that you have at least some good qualities to offer, you may feel more inclined to reach out to people.

People who can't like themselves often grew up having their flaws and shortcomings constantly pointed out by the adults around them. Those raised being scolded all the time also struggle to like themselves.

This doesn't change in adulthood. If you're scolded not just for a specific mistake but told that you fail at everything you do, it also becomes impossible to like yourself. Hearing consistent, harsh criticism about your work from a boss makes you believe you're incompetent, and therefore worthless. The same applies to interpersonal issues in the workplace: if you're told you always cause problems, you start thinking you're no good. People who are treated like this don't just lose confidence in getting along with others – they may start using internalised notions like 'I don't like myself' or 'I have no value' as reasons not to enter into relationships in the first place.

'If *you* don't like yourself, why would anyone else like you'? Thinking this way, you avoid stepping into relationships.

You might meet someone you like, only to find that you can't confess your feelings as you don't want to be hurt by rejection. To avoid the possibility of being rejected, you decide from the outset not to enter into the relationship at all.

People like this often think of themselves as gloomy. But it's not that they avoid relationships *because* they're gloomy. In reality, to avoid entering into relationships, they decide to *think* of themselves as gloomy – or, in Adler's words, as having no value. That way of thinking becomes the excuse that keeps them from stepping towards others.

It's true that interacting with people can sometimes lead to painful experiences. And in the workplace, unlike with friends, you can't choose who you deal with, so there's no avoiding engaging with people you dislike or find difficult.

But not everyone is unpleasant. People you think are difficult may not actually be so. And even if it's hard to build a good relationship right away with someone you've just met, what develops is rarely as scary as you imagine.

Fear of relationships isn't unique to you – the other person feels it, too. Someone always has to take the first step, which means you need the courage to enter into relationships yourself.

## Making Use of Who You Already Are

To step into relationships, you first have to realise that you've been using your own shortcomings as a self-made roadblock. It helps to consider that other people may not be as frightening as you imagine, but more important than that is changing how you see yourself. There's a reason I'm not saying *change yourself*, because that's far from easy. If you can make use of who you are right now, that, in the end, is what truly changes you.

As we've seen, once you like yourself, you can build strong relationships. But people who fear getting hurt decide that they can't afford to like themselves, and in doing so, they stay out of relationships – or at least avoid stepping into them proactively.

For example, someone who thinks of themselves as gloomy, and is told the same by others, can't readily become a cheerful person overnight. It's not impossible, but it's not easy. Even if they want to be more upbeat, they don't know what might happen once they change, so they can't bring themselves to suddenly become a stark contrast from the person they've always been.

To begin with, being a cheerful person isn't automatically better than the opposite. I've often said this to people who describe themselves as gloomy: 'Do you find that you're always worried about how your words and actions might come across to others?'

If they agree, I continue: 'Then at the very least, you've probably never intentionally hurt anyone, have you?'

I add the word *intentionally* because even when you don't mean to hurt someone, they can still be hurt by what you say or do.

To those who agree with this, I say: 'You call yourself gloomy, but you're so much more than that – you're kind.'

You may not be able to like a gloomy version of yourself, but couldn't you like a kind version?

Seen this way, it's far more realistic to think about how to make use of who you are right now. Instead of saying, 'I lack focus,' you could say, 'I'm good at distributing my attention.' Some people can focus well, but only when they're alone in a quiet place. In reality, ideal conditions for concentration aren't always available. Sometimes, you have to work in noisy environments with others or juggle multiple tasks at once. People who can do that are able to spread their attention.

Likewise, 'I get bored easily' sounds like a flaw, but it can also be seen as 'I'm decisive'. If you realise that the book you're reading isn't what you need right now and can decide to close it and pick up another, that's a strength.

As quoted earlier, Adler wrote that 'what matters is not what one is given, but how one uses what one has been given' (*Problems of Neurosis*). Thinking about how to use the traits you already possess is far easier than trying to become a different version of yourself.

It's also important not to set goals that are unattainable. For example, the goal of getting along with everyone can never be achieved. If you set an impossible goal like that, you end up comparing it to your current reality and using the fact that you can't get along with everyone as a reason not to enter into relationships at all.

Anyone who has firm beliefs is bound to clash with others every now and then. There's no need to deliberately say or do things that make people dislike you, but if, in spite of your efforts, some people *don't* think highly of you, that's merely proof that you're living freely, without pandering. When you come to that insight, you'll realise there's nothing to be gained in trying to be liked by everyone. And at that point, it won't bother you if you don't currently have anyone in your life who you would call a close friend.

When you can change how you see yourself in this way, you'll find that you're better able to accept yourself. When someone who has been avoiding relationships realises, 'I decided not to like myself so I wouldn't have to enter relationships,' they'll eventually come to accept themselves and gain the courage to connect.

## The Importance of Making Your Own Choices

To accept yourself, you also need to stop trying to live up to other people's standards.

As we've seen throughout the book so far, this kind of habit doesn't begin in adulthood. From a young age, many children try to live in a way that meets their parents' expectations.

A great many parents try to impose lofty ideals on their children, but no matter how disappointed any deviation from these might leave parents, children still need to live their own lives. Of course, there aren't many children with a strong enough sense of will to pursue their own path in defiance of their parents' wishes. Even as adults, many people continue trying to meet expectations with little idea of the kind of life they themselves want to live.

Parents often consult me about wanting to send their children to elite schools. I tell them that parents can't decide their children's lives, so the first step is to listen to what the child wants. But when parents say things like, 'If you go to a top school and get into a famous university, you'll succeed in life,' children sometimes buy into that idea. It's fine to hear other people's opinions when making decisions, but if you simply follow your parents' recommendations without question, it can't truly be said that you're making your own choices.

Many parents say, 'Children can't decide on their own. It's a parent's job to provide them with the best options.' Perhaps so. But while parents can try to lay down the tracks for their children's lives, the children still have to investigate and choose a direction for themselves.

Children often come to believe that a rosy future promised by their parents awaits them. But no matter how much they want to please their parents, they may not get good grades, or they may not get into the university their parents hoped for. And even if they *do* get accepted, that isn't the end – they still have to study after enrolling. When they stop getting good grades, some start acting out, skipping school or developing neuroses, all in an effort to regain their parents' attention.

As adults, some people start working to be liked by those around them, but when they fail to produce the desired results and stop getting attention, they become perpetually irritable, trying to get others to pay attention to them. Such people don't make decisions based on their own will – they choose their actions by constantly gauging others' *reactions*. They may want to believe such a way of living isn't self-centred, but in reality, they're abandoning all responsibility for their own lives.

Your life is yours to live. That means you have to think about *how* you want to live, regardless of your parents' or anyone else's expectations. Neither living the life your parents want in order to please them nor doing things that trouble them just to get their attention has any real meaning. You can't keep worrying about what others think; you have to decide your actions and your life based on your own free will.

Once, back when I was in elementary school, a friend called, inviting me to come over and play. The house I lived in was on the edge of the school district, about a thirty-minute walk from school for a child. I didn't have any friends nearby, so once I arrived home, I usually wouldn't go out again until the next school day. But when my friend called, I suddenly felt like going.

I asked my mother if it was okay for me to go. 'That's something you can decide for yourself,' I remember her saying at the time.

Back then, I thought you were supposed to ask your parents before going out. Maybe I believed that being a *good* child, the kind who always listened to their parents, would make them happy. Indeed, if my parents had told me to stay home, I wouldn't have gone against them. My mother's answer surprised me, and for the first time I felt the weight of deciding for myself, though I probably didn't know the word *responsibility* back then. Once you decide for yourself, you have to accept the outcome yourself – even if things don't turn out the way you hoped.

It wasn't a major life decision, so my mother probably felt no need to oppose it. But whether it's small, everyday choices or big decisions about your future, people who drag others into their decisions are really trying to avoid taking responsibility for deciding on their own.

# Don't Try to Become Special Just to Be Accepted

Not just in studying or work, but in every area of life, you need to have your own views and aim to become the person you want to be, regardless of how others see you or whether they approve of your actions. You may end up being recognised as producing better results than others, but there's no need to compete with people only for the express goal of earning recognition.

The Adlerian phrase 'striving for superiority' tends to imply being better than others by comparison, but excellence has nothing to do with competition. It also has nothing to do with trying to be seen as special. Being excellent simply means having acquired the knowledge and abilities necessary to achieve something.

People who aim for more than their actual capacity are, in a sense, straining to make themselves look bigger than they really are. This is the very definition of being habitually tense. Instead of going down that road, all you need to do is put in the effort to build your knowledge and skills.

The same applies to behaviour: you don't need to try to be special. Thinking that you won't be acknowledged unless you stand out is a sign of an inferiority complex. The corresponding pursuit of superiority is the attempt to be special by drawing everyone's attention.

I once knew someone who chose not to go on to high school, against his parents' wishes. Both of his parents were highly educated, so they couldn't imagine what it meant to start working right after graduating from middle school. I remember he rebelled hard in middle school – dyed his hair, shaved patterns into it and shaved his eyebrows.

One day, he said, 'I wouldn't have been able to get through to my parents if I hadn't acted that rebellious.' Of course, he could have talked to them without going to such extremes, but he believed that unless he was different from everyone else – unless he was special – his parents wouldn't listen to what he had to say.

When it comes to choosing a path in life, all you really need to think about is the kind of life you want to live. There's no need to choose one that confuses or troubles your parents just to oppose them.

If you deliberately choose a life your parents can't accept in order to upset them, you're still living bound by their expectations. To live your own life, you need to prioritise how *you* want to live. Your choices may confuse your parents, but there's no need to change your way of living because of that.

# Don't Be Afraid to Be Different
# from Everyone Else

As mentioned earlier, while some people try to be special, others try not to stand out, instead conforming to those around them. These are people who hesitate to live a life different from that of most others.

Even among those who want to be special, some aren't really trying to decide their own lives. They simply want to succeed in the same way everyone else does, and are satisfied living a similar kind of life. They believe that if their life differs too much from their perceived norm, they won't be recognised as special, and want to live according to a generally agreed-upon definition of what success looks like.

In truth, there's no need to act and live the same as everyone else. Kiyoshi Miki's concept of *eccentricity* can be a useful framework here. The adjective eccentric is often used negatively to mean out of the ordinary or off the rails, but Miki conceptualised eccentricity as *decentring*.

Here, the *centre* refers to common or conventional values. People who never question living the same way as everyone else are living at the centre. Such individuals don't ask themselves whether the way they're living is really right for them.

However, once you have an experience that shakes your sense of the world, you may no longer be able to remain at the centre. This can happen, for example, if you fall ill and can no longer work as you once did, or if you lose someone close to you – experiences that force you to re-examine values you once took for granted.

Even without such dramatic experiences, when you start to wonder whether it's really okay to keep living the way you are, you may be surprised to realise that you've never seriously thought about how you *want* to live – or you may notice that you've been deliberately avoiding such questions.

People who choose a life that departs from conventional values may look eccentric to others. When a child tries to live that way, parents who do live by conventional standards may oppose them.

Miki, however, had this to say:

*The capacity to become eccentric is a defining characteristic of human beings. That is precisely why, since ancient times, moderation – not too much, in balance, etc. – has so often been emphasised as the morality of everyday life.*

(On Shestovian Anxiety)

What Miki meant by eccentric isn't the *desire* to be special or different from everyone else. Rather, it means becoming free from existing standards and established values. Miki saw the ability to live eccentrically as a defining characteristic of human beings, and precisely because we have that capacity, societies since ancient times have emphasised moderation as a way of keeping everyday life workable.

If we consider why moderation has been emphasised throughout history, it becomes clear that humans have always had this freedom to depart from convention, and from that perspective, the desire to be special isn't unusual at all – it's an expression of that human freedom.

Still, the simple wish to be special doesn't mean an individual has actually moved away from the centre. People who want to be different, special and admired for it are still trapped by the centre, because they're craving recognition rather than living according to their own values.

Those who have truly stepped away from the centre don't think of themselves as special. They aren't obsessed with standing out or being recognised as superior. They simply hold views that differ from the majority, and they have the courage to express opinions that aren't the same as everyone else's.

# Have Confidence in Being Yourself

There are people who can explain who they are solely in terms of their attributes. They describe themselves only by naming the organisation they belong to, such as their company, or try to show off how superior they think they are by announcing their job title or academic background.

I used to offer counselling at psychiatric clinics, and the first session always began with self-introductions. It wasn't uncommon for people to be able to introduce themselves only through such attributes as titles and credentials.

As we've already seen in Chapter 4, attributes are things that belong to a person – like the 'beauty' in the phrase 'that person is beautiful' – but they aren't the person themselves. Your looks might fade, or illness might prevent you from moving your body freely, but those are simply changes in attributes – you don't stop being yourself. No one doubts that they are the same person today that they were as a child, even though their appearance has changed. The person themselves can also be described as their *personhood*.

Educational background, as we discussed on p. 64, is also just an attribute. People who introduce themselves by listing attributes sound as if they're reading their résumé out loud. But no matter how many attributes they list, you still don't know what kind of person they really are. That's because attributes aren't individuality – they're just traits shared with others.

. . .

When I was hospitalised after my heart attack, my only attribute was *patient*. In a hospital setting, your outside titles mean nothing. When people become ill, many suddenly realise that their life is finite, even though they had vaguely assumed they would live for many more years to come, and they begin to reconsider how they've lived their lives. Beyond that, they also come to see that their social titles lose all meaning once they're facing illness.

Becoming a patient doesn't mean that you've stopped being yourself or that you've lost your individuality. Still, some people find it hard to accept being placed in a situation where their social status no longer matters. Once you can accept this reality, however, it can be life changing.

Someone who could only define themselves through their attributes may, after an experience that brings them face to face with death, realise there's no need to prove their worth by talking about those things. Over time, they come to feel that they are their own unique person without mentioning them.

Others, however, can't reach that point. Unable to accept that they are just one patient among many, they bring up their social status, boast about how important they are and demand special treatment. Believing that you can only demonstrate your specialness – that you're more than just an average human being – through attributes like education, affiliation or position only proves that you don't believe that simply being yourself has any value.

I once heard a story about a man who had climbed the corporate ladder to become the president of a bank, and shortly afterwards suffered a stroke that left him unable to move freely. 'Kill me,' he begged his family, convinced that a body like his had no value anymore. You can imagine the distress that must have caused those dear to him.

How can someone in such a situation – deprived of their social status and removed from their usual circumstances – still believe their life has value? The answer is that there is value precisely in being alive. A newborn baby can't survive without help from its parents. Yet no one who sees that baby thinks, *This child has no inherent value*. On the contrary: simply seeing the child makes people happy. Adults, too, can think of themselves as contributing to those around them simply by being alive, even if they can't move freely.

If, through a radical life change beyond your control, you experience being free from social attributes and discover how liberating that can be, you may realise that you can't – and don't need to – go back to the way things were before.

# Embrace Individuality

When parents want their children to obey them and live *normal* lives, they may see any unusual traits as flaws to be corrected. The child may listen obediently to everything their parents say, stop causing trouble and become a *good* child who never pushes back. A child whose edges have all been smoothed away, however, becomes average – and *ordinary* in a sense very different from what I mean. Such a child may meet society's definition of 'good', but they live their life on a much smaller scale. When I talk about embracing ordinariness, I don't mean an average person whose edges have been smoothed away. Those edges shouldn't be seen as flaws – they should be recognised as strengths and left as they are.

What makes you different from everyone else – *that* is your individuality. You must be able to think, *I am me*, without any concern for how you differ from other people. In that sense, if you can accept your individuality and accept yourself as you are, you don't need to try to become special. You will naturally be different from others.

· · ·

Parents sometimes want their children to follow the same path they did, or they impose a path on them. Doctors and politicians may look at their children that way, eagerly planning to send them to medical school or a prestigious university if their grades allow for it. But such parents aren't paying attention to their child's individuality.

I mentioned earlier the story about Hideki Yukawa asking another professor to check his work (p. 110). In his autobiography, Yukawa said he wasn't a particularly noticeable child. His father, himself a scholar, originally intended for his children to become academics as well. But when he questioned whether becoming a scholar was the only way to be a worthy human being, he thought, *For Hideki, I need to consider a different way of life*, and tried to send him down an alternative path from his siblings. At that point, Yukawa's mother urged her husband to reconsider, insisting:

> *There are children who don't stand out. It isn't necessarily the flashy or precociously talented ones who go on to do outstanding work. On the contrary, it's often those who seem most unremarkable . . .*
>
> (*The Traveller*)

In truth, you can discover your individuality by yourself, but it is sometimes the people around you who discover it for you.

# An Irreplaceable Individuality

When parents recognise a sense of individuality in a child that none of their siblings has, the child often comes to see themselves as being uniquely distinct from their brothers or sisters. Even if parents don't notice it, when people around the child do, the child can discover aspects of their own individuality they were never aware of. If no one points it out, however, the child has no choice but to discover it on their own. To do that, they must be free from the fear of being different from those around them. They need to believe that they don't *have* to live a life identical to anyone else's.

True confidence doesn't come from being better than others by comparison. Confidence grows when you stop *trying* to be special, refuse to simply go along with that abstract notion of *everyone*, and think and act for yourself. Your parents can urge you in a certain direction, but you should pause and ask yourself whether you can live a life different from theirs and from everyone else's rather than blindly obeying.

To do that, you must turn your attention to your individuality — something no one else shares. Individuality doesn't fit into the framework of common attributes. As we've covered, academic background and even being good at your job are ultimately just attributes. People are constantly changing. Attributes may serve as indicators of how someone is at a given moment, but they aren't the person themselves, and losing them doesn't change a person's value. What remains the same, despite changes in outward appearance, is one's *personhood*.

When something can be reduced to a quantity, it can be compared and competed over. Qualitative things, like individuality, however, can't be compared or competed over. Those who can accept their own individuality won't feel the urge to compare or compete. Those who lack confidence, however, may try to compete with others in quantitative terms.

When you can feel that it's fine not to be special – not trying to beat others, not trying to attract attention, just being yourself without putting on a show or stretching to seem taller than you are – you'll find that life becomes so much easier to navigate.

## Stop Thinking Only of Yourself

It's no exaggeration to say that many of today's problems are caused by people who think only about themselves. But if you don't relate to others by competing, what should you do instead? You should cooperate with others. People who have lived their lives competing, however, often don't know what it means to live cooperatively.

There are people who are capable but not well liked by those around them. Such individuals often lack humility and may become defensive when their mistakes are pointed out to them, like the example we saw on p. 155. Because they think of themselves as special, simply having a mistake pointed out feels like an attack on their self-esteem. Those who are constantly preoccupied with how they're seen by others are ultimately interested only in themselves.

But this isn't the only type of capable person who isn't liked. When someone is overwhelmingly good at studying or work and insists on setting themselves apart from everyone else, others have no choice but to acknowledge their ability. At the same time, those others may develop an inferiority complex, thinking they can't compete no matter how hard they try. As a result, a talented person may be praised by the people around them, but not loved.

If that happens, it's not because the person is talented and others feel inferior. It's because, despite being capable, the person shows no willingness to cooperate. Again, they are interested only in themselves. Whether at school or in the workplace, no matter how adept someone is, if they don't try to work with others, they will quickly become isolated.

Cooperation can mean, for example, teaching. Yet some believe that teaching others – giving their knowledge to someone else – puts them at a disadvantage. Social psychologist Erich Fromm pointed out that such people think of *giving* as *giving up*, believing that if they give, they themselves will become poorer (*Man for Himself*).

The fact that there exist so many students who can only think about their own immediate gains must be considered a harmful consequence of social competition, and a failure of education. The same is true in the workplace. When a boss engages in blatant bullying or intimidation, people who are focused on protecting their own promotion prospects will look the other way. Such people, too, are interested only in themselves and won't try to help colleagues who are being harassed. When they themselves are caught in the crosshairs, they don't speak up or try to confront their superior, either.

• • •

As we saw on p. 66, Adler said that 'anyone can accomplish anything'. As Adler put it, this democratic principle that anyone can achieve anything through effort 'takes the wind out of the sails of so-called geniuses' (*The Science of Living*).

If this principle is accepted, those who see themselves as capable and are seen that way by others will stop being conceited. Those who believed their ability stems from innate talent will, once they understand that the real difference lies in effort, become even more diligent – precisely *because* they are humbler.

If this principle is not accepted, Adler said, people end up 'bearing the pressure of always being expected to perform, of constantly being pushed forward, and of being excessively preoccupied with themselves' (*The Science of Living*). After all, capable people who feel the pressure of expectation aren't driven by a sense of mission – they want to be seen favourably by others. In that sense, they are ultimately concerned only with themselves.

## Taking an Interest in Others and Working Together

Learning to direct your interest not only towards yourself, but towards other people as well, will make you better able to share your knowledge with them. At that point, you will no longer fear that it might put you at a disadvantage or that the people you teach may one day surpass you. If someone you've taught goes on to outperform you, that's merely proof of your skill as an educator.

If students fail to grow despite being taught, it cannot be said that their teacher is competent. When students don't achieve good results, it usually isn't because they were lazy about studying – in reality, the problem lies in how they were taught.

In that sense, managers in the workplace are also teachers, because they're responsible for teaching their colleagues knowledge and skills. A manager may give their knowledge generously, but they don't become poorer for it. On the contrary, unless their colleagues grow and eventually surpass them, the manager can't be said to have performed their job as an educator. Junior colleagues surpass their bosses precisely because the boss is a good educator.

By contrast, managers who hinder their juniors' growth are competing with them. Scolding with reprimands like 'You always mess up,' or 'Nothing you do ever works,' drains even capable people of their motivation, with the tacit goal of preventing them from being seen as better than their boss.

Adler said that rather than getting in people's way to remain the centre of attention, 'it takes far more courage to help others' (*The Pattern of Life*).

A boss who insists on being the sole centre of attention and obstructs their staff members' growth does nothing for the organisation. When junior colleagues fail or cannot improve, the boss needs to step in and help educate them. By doing this, they create a sense of contribution – and with this sense of contribution, they come to feel joy in working together. As people grow, competition fades into the background and they are freed from a life of habitual tension.

People who can direct their interest towards others can *give* to others – those who are interested only in themselves cannot. Adler put it this way:

> *When vanity grows stronger, people think more*
> *about themselves than about others, and they forget*
> *what life demands of them and what they must give*
> *as human beings.*

> (*Understanding Human Nature*)

People who are preoccupied with making themselves look good think only about themselves, have no real interest in others and don't try to give.

• • •

There is a Latin proverb that goes *dum docent discunt*: 'while they teach, they learn'. It means that by teaching, you also learn yourself. After all, you cannot teach something unless you truly understand it. Teaching allows you to check your own level of comprehension and to discover where your grasp is still incomplete. Anyone who has ever taught knows this.

We saw earlier that capable people can sometimes make others feel inferior. Those who take an interest in others and contribute by teaching, however, are loved, and don't become isolated.

Those on the receiving end of teaching need not feel ashamed about learning. The teacher simply acquired knowledge earlier and, through effort, developed the proficiency to teach. When learners understand this, they come to believe that they, too, can do the same if they put in the hard work.

Society shouldn't be built around the idea of there being only a small number of excellent people while everyone else feels inferior in comparison, losing their motivation to contribute. The ideal organisation is one where knowledgeable people teach others so that the group as a whole can grow.

When everyone cooperates, everyone improves, not just the capable few. Instead of competing, all those involved – including supervisors – should acquire knowledge and work together to approach their work with genuine motivation.

In this way, it's important for people who once cared only about themselves to redirect their pursuit of excellence in the right direction by helping raise up others.

## Winning Alone Is Meaningless

Some people think that not only studying and work but life itself is a competition. Such individuals can't understand what it means to step off the competitive stage. Once you free yourself from the yardstick of winning and losing, life starts to look different.

Those who step away from competition find that it's not nearly as frightening as they might have imagined. This doesn't mean they feel nothing when they lose; rather, when they study and work without a mind for winning or losing, they stop being driven by fear of defeat and no longer live in constant anxiety that although they are winning now, they might end up losing in the future.

In Ryunosuke Akutagawa's short story 'The Spider's Thread', the protagonist Kandata clings to a silver thread hanging down from heaven, trying to climb from hell into paradise. As he climbs higher and glances down, he sees countless other sinners climbing after him. The thread is thin enough that it could break under just one person's weight, and Kandata convinces himself that it couldn't possibly bear so many. Thinking this, he shouts:

'The thread is mine!'

At that instant, his lifeline snaps. The Buddha, who had been watching all along, turns away filled with sorrow.

When you compete, everyone ends up plunging together into the abyss. Even if you manage to win, the fact that there *is* a winner means that there are losers at the same time. Those on the winning side push themselves harder, but those on the other side lose their motivation altogether. From an overall perspective, the gains and losses cancel out. And because work is something we accomplish together rather than alone, that loss of motivation drags down the whole group, turning the result into a net loss.

# Gaining a Sense of Belonging

Feeling that you belong to some kind of community is one of our fundamental needs as human beings. On this, Adler said:


*Our desire always to be connected with the community, to believe that we are connected – or at least to appear to be connected – gives rise to distinctive ways of living, thinking, and action.*

(*Understanding Human Nature*)

Merely *belonging* to a community doesn't necessarily make you feel *connected* to it, yet a sense of connection can be gained by simply playing a part in things. This doesn't necessarily mean you have to do anything extraordinary.

For example, when a child is born, the family changes. Even without actively *doing* anything, a child has the power to transform the family. Parents can hardly remember how they lived before the child was born.

The same is true for adults. When you start a job at a new company, that company naturally existed before you arrived – but once you've joined, the company as it was before you is effectively gone. Just as a child unquestionably changes a family, a new employee also changes a company. In that sense, you don't need to worry about adapting yourself to the company, because everything is always changing anyway.

Unlike a new baby, however, adults can change a community not only by their very existence, but also through their actions. We've already seen that in workplaces where the atmosphere makes it difficult to voice new ideas, there are likely people who have long thought something was wrong but lacked the courage to speak up. If, for instance, you think your boss is saying something unreasonable, and instead of silently complying, you point out what seems wrong with it, the company too will change. It is when someone starts doing what no one has done before that the workplace changes.

Even if it's not about raising objections, you can change an organisation by proposing ideas that no one has thought of in the past. Of course, new ideas often meet resistance due to a lack of precedent. You may avoid major losses if you only do what has already been proven successful, but you will never produce innovation, such as the kind that creates bestsellers or long-term successes. Taking on something new always involves risk, but if you fear change and focus only on avoiding losses, the organisation will never develop. This applies not only to people who work in organisations – everyone has the power to change the community they belong to.

# It Isn't Give and Take

In order to change an organisation, you don't need to compete with other people. Organisations change through cooperation, not rivalry, and something as simple as responding when someone asks you for advice can be enough to make a difference.

There are scenarios where you may see someone who is asking you for help as a challenger, so helping feels like you're taking a loss. If your advice enables someone else to succeed, you might even feel as though you've inexplicably been outdone.

As we've already seen, however, giving isn't a loss. People who think giving puts them at a disadvantage can only see the world in terms of give and take. They're always keeping score: 'I did this much for you, so you owe me that much in return.' When someone like that happens, one day, to give without expecting anything back, they may experience an unexpected feeling of joy. That feeling is what's called a sense of contribution.

Even people who have always believed that giving is a loss can eventually come to feel that joy. And once they see for themselves how good it feels to give without expecting anything in return, their perspective changes.

Indeed, what you give may not come back to you directly from the person you gave it to. But people who share what they know with those around them freely will, when they themselves need help, receive it from someone else. After all, in a community where everyone gives what they can to others, help eventually comes back around.

In spite of this truth, there are always those who think only about receiving from others. People like this may find someone who is willing to help them, but if they take what they get for granted and never try to give back, it's entirely possible that one day they will look around and find no one left beside them.

It's also a mistake to give to others with the explicit aim of getting something back. When giving to others brings you a sense of contribution, you can indeed feel that you have value, but it's wrong to intentionally set out to be useful to others for that reason. Just as capable people don't boast about their competence, they ought to learn to give naturally, without calculation.

To make this possible, when someone asks you for something, don't immediately think, *I can't do that*, or *Why are they always asking* me? Instead, just try saying yes. If you're someone who is used to always expecting something in return, it's difficult to stop assuming you deserve payback. But the next time someone asks you for help, try accepting their request with an open heart, and pay attention to how it makes you feel.

• • •

As we said on p. 203, a sense of belonging is one of our basic human needs; but it's important to remember that belonging to a community and being at its centre aren't the same thing at all. People who believe they are the centre of their community become dissatisfied when others don't behave according to their expectations. However, the fact that others don't do as you expect is no reason to be angry. If you have the right to live your life as you please, without regard for other people's expectations, then you must grant them the same right.

# Use Your Talents to Contribute to Others

To be able to cooperate with others, it isn't enough to think merely about your position within the community – you must also think about the *active role* you play in community life. That role differs from person to person, but capable people should fulfil theirs by using their individual talents for the sake of others.

I've used the word *talent*, but as we have seen, both Adler and I believe that this isn't a matter of some people being talented and others not. With the appropriate education and effort, we know that anyone can achieve anything (see p. 67).

Those who think only of using the abilities they've acquired for themselves are chasing personal superiority, and seek satisfaction by having others acknowledge how capable they are. What Adler called personal superiority, however, isn't pursued purely as a private matter. It can also include the desire not to lose out to peers such as classmates and colleagues – so interpersonal factors are involved as well.

For instance, there are people who say they absolutely *must* get into the top university of the moment, or who absolutely *must* become a doctor. For such people, what matters isn't actual ability, but the academic credentials they think prove that ability. These are the people who see value in having graduated from a famous university only as a way to beat their peers. Because their effort is going into chasing status rather than developing real ability, that energy needs to be redirected.

When people like this, who care only about themselves, realise that their efforts won't be rewarded, they often stop trying to overcome difficult challenges. Those who, on the other hand, take an interest in others and seek to contribute to them won't stop making an effort – no matter how difficult the task may be. This kind of effort may sound like self-sacrifice, but you'll find that it's nothing of the sort. For example, if your goal in studying for entrance exams is simply to earn a medical licence at a university, your motivation won't last. Without a motive such as wanting to help the sick, it would be difficult to continue working as a doctor – not just to become one, but to *remain* one.

While I was taking care of my father, who was suffering from dementia, the doctor we were working with would rush over whenever called, even in the middle of the night or on his days off. He never seemed grim or worn down; if anything, he looked like he enjoyed being there to help. That attitude is only possible when one takes pleasure in the simple act of contributing to others.

I once heard that some students who enter elite high schools start talking almost immediately about whether they will go on to the University of Tokyo, Kyoto University or medical school after graduating. At some schools, as many as one third of students from each class go on to medical school. It's true that society would be in trouble if no one became a doctor – but it's also true that not everyone with good grades needs to become one. Those who enter medical school without thinking about what they'll actually do as doctors are usually using their talents only to prove themselves.

Of course, even after becoming a doctor, you still have to continue studying. Medicine advances day by day, and constant learning is essential in order to save patients' lives. If that study is done solely to come out on top in an imagined competition, it will be painful going. But studying in order to save patients' lives won't feel like a trial at all. Saving a patient's life isn't always easy, but when you manage to pull it off, it brings a profound sense of contribution, through which you feel a clear sense of your own worth.

All this being said, becoming a doctor for the sake of status is also a mistake. When people are driven by vanity, work becomes painful. They try to make themselves look good, but if they lack sufficient ability, they fail to meet the expectations others have of them. As a result, they become habitually tense, and true confidence remains forever out of reach.

•  •  •

I've repeatedly discussed the harm caused by competition, in that it keeps you trapped in comparison and anxiety. But once you can feel that you are contributing to others, there's no longer any need to compare yourself or chase after victory. In fact, once you've found true confidence, that constant sense of urgency and anxiety will slip away.

# You Contribute Simply by Existing

I've been thinking about what it means to contribute, and I want to make one thing very clear: you don't have to be special to make a difference. Yes, some people have an impact through high-profile achievements, but the ways in which a person can contribute to their community are as diverse as people themselves.

When you're young, you're unlikely to experience a noticeable decline in your abilities day to day, but anyone can face illness or injury that limits physical movement. The important thing to remember is that even if your body fails you or you can no longer work, it doesn't erase your value, or your ability to contribute.

Take the cellist Jacqueline du Pré, for example. She was struck by multiple sclerosis at the age of twenty-eight, suddenly losing sensation in her arms and fingers during a performance  After a long struggle with the disease, she passed away at forty-two.

Yet du Pré didn't live her too-short life crushed by misfortune. True, after her diagnosis, she could no longer perform as a cellist in the way she once had; yet she found ways to remain on stage – as a percussionist, or narrating Prokofiev's *Peter and the Wolf.* She continued to perform as much as she could.

It may seem like an exceptional case, but many people experience a detour from the path they wanted to take. A researcher may end up in a commercial industry because labs are limited, or a promising athlete may have their dreams dashed by injury. Even then, there are always ways to contribute, even if it's not the path you originally envisioned. You don't have to cling to just one road.

There is a part of *you* that doesn't change, no matter what happens. Being able to move freely or work is an attribute – something that belongs to a person but isn't the person in and of itself. As we explored on p. 64, you can take off one hat and put on another, but you don't become a different person.

People have value simply by existing. That is, on the level of existence, you are enough just the way you are.

Someone who has contributed through work doesn't lose their inherent worth if illness or age prevents them from continuing to do so. They've simply stopped contributing through work.

Today, many people treat worth as something earned through constant doing. Some assume they'll always be able to work and dismiss those who can't. Yet even they know that a child or an ageing parent brings joy simply by being alive, regardless of ability.

For those who have always measured worth by being able to do something, it might be hard to believe that just being alive counts as contributing. But consider when a family member or close friend is hospitalised: even if their condition isn't perfect, just knowing they're alive is a relief and a joy. The same principle applies to you. No one thinks you are without value just because you can no longer work.

We've discussed feelings of inferiority, and one reason people feel 'less than' is thinking they're not contributing through action. But life itself isn't something that can be measured by comparison. No matter how you live, your mere existence contributes to others, and that alone gives you value.

Contributing by being alive also means that the mere act of sharing space with others has an effect. People can't exist in total isolation. In daily life, consciously or unconsciously, we are influenced by those around us.

Take a crowded train, for instance. People get closer than they ever would in normal life, prompting them to look out the window or bury themselves in their phones to show indifference. Even when seats are empty, a neighbour can create a sense of discomfort. These situations illustrate how simply occupying the same space affects others.

The same holds true in workplaces or at home. One bad-tempered person can create tension, while a cheerful person can ease it. Just by being there, and without doing anything special, you contribute to others and to the collective atmosphere.

Indeed, mere presence is a form of non-verbal interaction. Your energy shapes the environment and mood around you, even without words or actions. You play a role in the community simply by being there, contributing in your own way.

# The Important Things in Life

Even if you can't change the competitive society you're being forced to live in, you can still make the conscious decision not to compete. People who fixate on winning obsess over victory and defeat, but both are beside the point. Your work may be evaluated, but failing to earn a high rating doesn't mean you lost.

Competition is meaningless, because what truly matters in life isn't beating others and achieving quantitative success. I doubt there's anyone who's never asked themselves what really matters in life, but some people who have enjoyed smooth sailing may deliberately avoid that question.

. . .

Once, I wrote in a manuscript, 'I'm sure there isn't anyone who has never woken in the middle of the night with a pounding heart, thinking they had come close to death'. Later, I was shocked to see an editor pencil in, 'I haven't'.

That editor was successful at work, so I couldn't help but wonder. Had they really never thought, even once, that there might be something more important than success? Or was it that the thought *did* arise from time to time, but whenever it did, they shoved it aside, telling themselves not to question such things?

I once saw a TV interview featuring a man in his seventies who had just lost his wife. 'Frankly,' he said, 'I wish I had spent more time with my family. In the end, work didn't matter at all.' While we all have to work to make a living, for this man, losing his wife made him realise there are more important considerations to keep in mind.

He may well have pondered the meaning of life when he was younger. But amid a busy life, I suspect he sealed off the question of what truly mattered to him. Why exactly do so many of us do this? Because even those who have worked hard their whole lives fear that if they start wondering, *Is it really okay to live like this?* The spell will break. They'll lose the will to work – maybe even the will to go on living.

Even those who have made career success their life goal might hear this story and think, *Maybe I, too, got so wrapped up in work that I lost sight of what mattered most.*

• • •

When I talk with young people who come to me for counselling about what really matters to them, they usually accept my advice without resistance. Few of them would say they've been successful in life – most have faced some kind of setback. That's probably why they encountered life's truths early. They don't yet know how to live, so we end up talking it through slowly. You might say the reason they can accept my advice so readily is that they have nothing to lose.

By contrast, people with elite educations and a track record of success often understand what I tell them but find themselves unable to accept it. Maybe they don't want to. Accepting it might trap them in the thought, *So what was my life up to now?*

Of course, I'm not saying what they achieved was meaningless; those achievements mattered because of how they contributed to others. The important thing to remember is that your value is not determined by the ability to contribute through work, and it is not defined by other people's opinions. To see that, you have to focus not on the work, but on the contribution.

• • •

Even if the way you contribute changes – whether in response to feedback or to changing circumstances – if you can believe that simply being alive is a contribution in and of itself, you won't feel that you've been rendered worthless.

# Living Happily

What matters in life isn't competition or success. Put simply, it's happiness.

I once met a young man who decided to quit almost immediately after joining a company, without even waiting for the May holidays (Japan's 'Golden Week', which comes about a month after new employees start work in April). Asked why, he said he had been forced into a cold-call sales role and had yet to land a contract. He had been a straight-A student his whole life and had never faced setbacks. It was clear that this first failure at work hit him hard.

But that wasn't the only reason he quit. He added, 'When I looked at my boss, he didn't look happy at all. Sure, the pay was good. I could buy a house at a younger age than most people. But I might have died from overwork. That would make everything meaningless. I can't live without working, but I don't live in order to work. If I don't feel happy while working, what's the point?'

That was how he saw it. If his boss had looked happy, he might not have quit.

At the time, he may have simply sensed that his boss was unhappy, and having read this far, you'll know why he felt that way. His boss was habitually tense, always obsessed with winning and succeeding in competition.

. . .

So, how can we live happily?

**First, step out of the competition**. Most of us are taught by our parents and adult role models how to win, but not what to do when we lose.

Those who have never lost are often the least able to recover when they finally do. Words of encouragement like 'try harder next time' don't help, because they believe losing at some task means they are without value. But whether you win or lose, your value doesn't drop. Once you believe that, there's no need to live on edge, and happiness becomes possible. Life will throw you challenges far tougher than winning competitions. Those who studied relentlessly and passed elite exams will later face jobs that demand more than any test ever did. They may succeed at work and still struggle with relationships. Children may act in ways that worry their parents. Partnerships may sour.

When that happens, your once-sunny future suddenly feels like it has gone dark. That's precisely when you need the strength to push through difficulty. And to build that strength, you mustn't see life as a competition.

**Second, you must recognise that the key to happiness is cooperation.** When you cooperate with others, you gain a sense of contribution. Unlike the fragile confidence that comes only from beating others and vanishes the moment you lose, the confidence born of contribution is unshakeable.

# CONCLUSION

## Finding the Courage to Be Ordinary

# People with Real Confidence Don't Rush

I hope that what you've read in these pages has given you some direction for how to live.

I've talked about adults who chase after success and being special. But even if you don't become special, even if you never succeed, all you can do is live in the moment – relaxed, attentive and steady, day by day.

There's confidence you should have, and confidence you shouldn't. The truly capable don't boast about their abilities. They don't even say they're confident. They simply put in the necessary effort and face the task at hand. The kind of confidence that makes you want to brag is the unhealthy kind you should let go of. Bragging happens when your attention is fixed on others.

What does healthy confidence look like? Adler put it this way:

*Those who have confidence and are able to confront life's tasks do not become impatient.*

(Social Interest: A Challenge to Mankind)

Confident people don't run away from hard problems. They face life's tasks without bringing in anxiety or excuses. *That's* what healthy confidence looks like.

People with healthy confidence don't stretch themselves thin or try to look better than they are. They start from where they are now, make the necessary effort and take on their own life tasks.

They also know that evaluations or assessments and their own inherent value are two different things. Even if your boss chews you out, that's merely their personal judgement – it isn't necessarily right. Those with healthy confidence can brush off criticism without feeling discouraged. Even after failure, they keep trying, pushing forward without worrying about what other people think.

## Being an Ordinary Person

Writing this book prompted me to look back on my own life, and I realised I spent years trying – and failing – to be special, dragging that frustration along wherever I went. I wanted to be special because I couldn't accept myself as I was: ordinary.

As I wondered what it means to live ordinarily, without trying to impress, I recalled a story often told about Adler.

Before meeting him, Phyllis Bottome, a writer and friend of Adler's, expected to find 'a genius like Socrates' (Edward Hoffman, *The Drive for Self*). But when she actually met Adler, what he said was nothing remarkable. She was left deeply disappointed.

What Bottome had expected, perhaps, was a charismatic figure. But later, when she heard Adler speak about war, she no longer thought of him as an ordinary person.

Adler's ideas didn't come across as special. There's a story about someone who attended a lecture of his complaining, 'Isn't everything he said just common sense?' Yet ideas that may seem obvious at first can completely change a person's life. They may not resonate initially, but later, when you're struggling, their true relevance to your life suddenly becomes clear.

There's another anecdote from one of Adler's lectures. As the start time approached and he hadn't appeared, the organisers grew anxious. It turned out Adler had arrived long before, taking a seat in the front row. No one had noticed. That, too, speaks volumes about the person he was.

Socrates, whom Bottome mentioned, may also have looked like any old man if he had stayed quiet. But even then, instead of dazzling people with jargon or verbal sparring when he did talk, he spoke in everyday language, and his words went straight to the heart.

What these stories show is that truly exceptional people don't feel the need to see themselves as special or to lord it over others. Adler didn't dress himself up – he simply gave everything he had to the task in front of him. That seemingly ordinary stance gave courage and solace to countless people.

• • •

You don't need to be special.

You don't need to flaunt charisma or put on a show of flamboyance.

All you need to do is face your own tasks sincerely. That alone is enough to influence others, create meaningful contributions and, in time, enrich your life.

# WORKS CITED


Adler, Alfred. *Adler Speaks: The Lectures of Alfred Adler*. Mark H. Stone and Karen A. Drescher eds. New York: iUniverse Inc., 2004.

———. *Der Sinn des Lebens* (*Social Interest: A Challenge to Mankind*). Wien/Leipzig: Verlag Dr. Rolf Passer, 1933.

———. *The Education of Children*. London: George Allen & Unwin, 1930.

———. *Individualpsychologie in der Schule* (*Individual Psychology in the School*). Leipzig: S. Hirzel, 1929.

———. *Menschenkenntnis* (*Understanding Human Nature*). Leipzig: S. Hirzel, 1927.

———. *The Pattern of Life*. New York: Cosmopolitan Book Corporation, 1930.

———. *Problems of Neurosis*. Routledge, Trench, Trubner & Co., 1929.

———. *The Science of Living*. New York: Garden City Publishing Co., 1929.

———. *Schwer erziehbare Kinder* (*Children with Behavioural Problems*). In Adler, Alfred. *Psychotherapie und Erziehung Band I* (*Psychotherapy and Education Volume I*). Frankfurt: Fischer Taschenbuch Verlag, 1982.

———. *What Life Should Mean to You*. Boston: Little, Brown, 1931.

Akutagawa, Ryunosuke. 'Kumo no ito' ('The Spider's Thread'). *Akai Tori*, July 1918.

Fromm, Erich. *Man for Himself: An Inquiry into the Psychology of Ethics.* New York: Rinehart & Company, 1947.

Guitton, Jean. *Mon testament philosophique (My Philosophical Testament).* Paris: Presses de la Renaissance, 1997.

Hegel, Georg Wilhelm Friedrich. *Grundlinien der Philosophie des Rechts (Elements of the Philosophy of Right).* Berlin: Nicolaische Buchhandlung, 1821.

Hoffman, Edward. *The Drive for Self: Alfred Adler and the Founding of Individual Psychology.* Boston: Da Capo Press, 1994.

Manaster, Guy J. et al. eds. *Alfred Adler: As We Remember Him.* Chicago: North American Society of Adlerian Psychology, 1977.

Miki, Kiyoshi. *Katararezaru tetsugaku (Unspoken Philosophy).* Tōkyō: Kōdansha gakujutsu bunko, 1977.

————. *Jinseiron nōto (Notes on the Theory of Life).* ōsaka: Sōgensha, 1947.

————. 'Shesutofuteki fuan ni tsuite' ('On Shestovian Anxiety'). In Miki, Kiyoshi, *Gakumon to jinsei (Learning and Life).* Tōkyō: Chūō Kōronsha, 1947.

Rilke, Rainer Maria. *Briefe an einen jungen Dichter (Letters to a Young Poet).* Leipzig: Insel Verlag, 1929.

Tsurumi, Shunsuke. *Otona ni naru tte nani? (What Does It Mean to Grow Up?).* Tōkyō: Shōbunsha, 2002.

Umehara, Takeshi. *Warai no kōzō (The Structure of Laughter).* Tōkyō: Kadokawa Shoten, 1972.

Yukawa, Hideki. *Tabibito (The Traveller).* Tōkyō: Asahi Shimbunsha, 1958.